Thinking and Learning about Mathematics in the Early Years

How can early years practitioners help young children to become not only numerate but also aspiring mathematicians who love numbers, shapes and mathematical comparisons?

The introduction of the Foundation Stage has led to practitioners seeking ways to teach maths that are more in line with the creative and playful ways young children learn other subjects.

Linda Pound draws on current thinking about children's mathematical development to show how you can encourage and enhance the numeracy skills of any child in the early years by linking maths to everyday life situations and making it a playful and enjoyable cross-curricular activity.

This highly practical and engaging text includes chapters on:

- ▶ why maths is often seen as 'hard' and what practitioners can do to help young children be more successful
- ▶ exploring shapes, space, measures and patterns
- ▶ how to make maths more fun and playful, using games, humour, stories and rhymes
- ▶ using music and dance to enhance mathematical understanding
- ▶ encouraging children to see the connection between maths and everyday experiences through, for example, sorting, matching and guessing
- ▶ creating an environment for mathematical development, indoors and out.

Concluding with a chapter on how practitioners and parents can become more confident in their use of maths, this user-friendly text, packed full of ideas, is essential reading for practitioners in any early years setting. Students on Early Education courses will also find much here to inspire them.

Linda Pound is an Early Years Education consultant and a regular contributor to *Nursery World*.

The Nursery World/Routledge Essential Guides for Early Years Practitioners

Books in this series, specially commissioned and written in conjunction with *Nursery World* magazine, address key issues for early years practitioners working in today's nursery and school environments. Each title is packed full of practical activities, support, advice and guidance, all of which are in line with current government early years policy. The authors use their experience and expertise to write accessibly and informatively, emphasising through the use of case studies the practical aspects of the subject, whilst retaining strong theoretical underpinnings throughout.

These titles will encourage the practitioner and student alike to gain greater confidence and authority in their day-to-day work, offering many illustrative examples of good practice, suggestions for further reading and many invaluable resources. For a handy, clear and inspirational guide to understanding the important and practical issues, the early years practitioner or student need look no further than this series.

Thinking and Learning about Mathematics in the Early Years

Linda Pound

Routledge
Taylor & Francis Group

LONDON AND NEW YORK

NURSERY
WORLD

First published 2008
by Routledge
2 Park Square, Milton Park, Abingdon, Oxon OX14 4RN

Simultaneously published in the USA and Canada
by Routledge
270 Madison Ave, New York, NY 10016

Routledge is an imprint of the Taylor & Francis Group, an informa business

Typeset in Perpetua by
Florence Production Ltd, Stoodleigh, Devon
Printed and bound in Great Britain by
Antony Rowe Ltd, Chippenham, Wilts

British Library Cataloguing in Publication Data
A catalogue record for this book is available from the British Library

Library of Congress Cataloging in Publication Data
Pound, Linda.
  Thinking and learning about maths in the early years/Linda
  Pound. – 1st ed.
     p. cm. – (The nursery world/Routledge essential guides
     for early years practitioners)
  Includes bibliographical references and index.
  1. Mathematics – Study and teaching (Early childhood).
  I. Title.
  QA135.6.P67 2008
  372.7 – dc22   2007040791

ISBN10: 0–415–43235–9 (hbk)
ISBN10: 0–415–43236–7 (pbk)
ISBN10: 0–203–92878–4 (ebk)

ISBN13: 978–0–415–43235–1 (hbk)
ISBN13: 978–0–415–43236–8 (pbk)
ISBN13: 978–0–203–92878–3 (ebk)

Contents

Tables

Introduction

This book is about young children's mathematical development. The area of learning and development that practitioners have been accustomed to thinking of as *mathematical development* in the foundation stage has been closely linked to *mathematics* or *numeracy* in the National Curriculum and Primary National Strategy for numeracy. With the publication of the *Early Years Foundation Stage* (EYFS) (DfES 2007), practitioners are now having to get used to calling the same set of early learning goals Problem-solving, Reasoning and Numeracy (PSRN). However, whatever the name of the area of learning and development, there are a number of issues associated with it. In addition, practitioners who work with children up to the age of three will be used to thinking about development in the way outlined in *Birth to Three Matters* (Sure Start Unit 2002). The framework's focus on

▶   a strong child
▶   a skilful communicator
▶   a competent learner, and
▶   a healthy child.

has now to be merged with ways of thinking about the growth of children's understanding in terms of the areas of learning and development.

This book will focus on the importance of making mathematics in the early years playful and cross-curricular. Many books about maths aimed at early years practitioners talk mostly about what adults will do. The part that children play in that process (with the support of adults) is often neglected. In this book the emphasis is on the value of child-initiated activity. This book will also underline the value of practitioners working closely with parents and carers since they know their own children best, and their involvement in learning is invaluable, in mathematics as in all other areas of learning and development.

The first three chapters look at general issues surrounding mathematics and young children – considering what happens in real life; what is known about how mathematics is learnt, and what is likely to improve the effectiveness of mathematics education. It begins to consider what practitioners can do to support children's understanding. Chapter 4 looks at pattern; Chapter 5 at the role of playful teaching and learning; Chapter 6 considers the development of mathematical thinking. In Chapter 7 the role of communication – talking and listening – in developing mathematical understanding is explored, while in Chapter 8 the role of creative media in supporting mathematical thinking and learning is reviewed. Chapter 9 focuses on creating an environment to support mathematical development. The final chapter considers the vital importance of parents and professionals working together in order to support children becoming mathematicians.

Chapter 1

Is maths hard?

The key to being able to do mathematics is wanting to.

(Devlin 2000: 254)

In this chapter you will:

▶ consider what it is that makes maths appear to be a hard subject;
▶ examine some of the research evidence about our inborn mathematical abilities;
▶ review some of the things that practitioners do with young children that make mathematics easier or more difficult for them to learn.

Most people regard maths as a hard subject. Ask any group of people what they think about maths and the majority will tell you that they were never good at it; that they cannot manage their own financial affairs; or indeed that they leave that sort of thing to someone else. Perhaps they will say that they liked (or didn't like) it at school until they had a particular teacher. Professor Keith Devlin (2000), himself a mathematician, supports the idea that it is a hard subject. He reports on a furore that arose when a Barbie doll was marketed that said among other things 'Maths is hard'. Those who complained argued that it was hard enough to encourage girls to be interested in the subject and that this doll simply made matters worse. The manufacturers responded by changing the phrase spoken by the doll to 'Maths is not hard, just different'. Although agreeing that nothing should be done to make maths less attractive to children (or adults), Devlin writes that the manufacturers were wrong to change the wording. He maintains that maths *is* hard because although humans have an instinctive ability to use mathematical understanding in the real world it requires our brains to:

▶ apply that understanding to reasoning about an imaginary or abstract world; and moreover

▶ develop logical and rigorous proof of that reasoning.

These are things that the human brain finds difficult. We use our innate mathematical understanding in our everyday lives to cross the street or to cook a meal, but it requires a different kind of thinking to apply our natural instincts or abilities to things that do not exist. When a young child holds a sweet or a toy in each hand, the objects are real and tangible. If you watch a very young child wrestling with this concept of two and more you will see him or her shifting the objects from hand to hand – putting one down, picking up another, putting them in the other hand and generally contriving to put more than two objects into two hands.

The development of abstract thought occurs over time. As they get older children can think about other sweets or toys in a bag or cupboard. They do not actually have to hold or see the objects in order to think about how many, or how few, there are and whether there will be enough for them and their friends. But maths as a subject requires children to consider abstract concepts such as whether two is less or more than three and whether three plus two is less or more than four, or perhaps the same. It requires us to learn how to think about numbers or quantities (such as billions of miles) that are described as beyond imagining; or fractions of whole numbers (nanoseconds) so tiny as to be unthinkable. It even requires us to learn to think about numbers or quantities that *could* not exist (Mazur 2003). The more extreme these numbers or quantities become the more we need to understand the processes by which we were able to think about small, imaginable, everyday examples.

Similarly, although the human brain is very good at estimating and at identifying patterns that can be generalised, it is less good at coming up with accurate answers. Crossing the road, for example, involves estimating the speed of oncoming traffic, the potential speed of walking (or running), the distance to be covered and the time needed to cross the road safely. This calculation and many others at least as complex are undertaken every day, many times a day. And they all rest on our guesses or estimates, which in turn rely on our experience, the pattern of previous events and experiences. Most of the maths we do in our everyday lives is of this nature and yet the popular view of mathematics, heavily underlined by our own experiences in school, is that right answers are what really count in maths. In fact, mathematical discovery relies on the same guesswork that informs our everyday maths. The need for accurate, precise answers comes later as mathematicians set out to prove their hunches. The detailed work required for this proof is not something that comes so easily to the human brain. However, 'doing mathematics does not require any special ability not possessed by every one of us' (Devlin 2000: 253). In short, although mathematical thinking may be challenging for our brains, the only things that separate great mathematicians from ordinary people struggling to sort out the household bills or complete their maths homework are:

▶ coping with creating and holding on to a range of complex abstract ideas;
▶ the level of insight or understanding which can be applied to those ideas; and
▶ skill and practice in being able to back up hunches or insights with logical explanations.

(Devlin 2000)

It would be possible to leave it at that, to accept that maths is a hard subject and that it will always be a struggle to use our mathematical understanding in everyday life. But understanding and applying maths is important in all sorts of ways and for all sorts of reasons. It may be as simple as not wanting to be cheated when we go shopping or not wanting to waste time or money buying more wallpaper than we need or taking a longer route than is necessary. Understanding maths enables people to withstand misleading statistics or false claims by advertisers. If we are to support children in becoming autonomous learners and responsible citizens then it is the role of educators to ensure that children feel as comfortable with numbers as they do with words. Not being comfortable with numbers is as disempowering in our society as not being able to read.

WHAT MAKES MATHS EASIER?

Fortunately, despite the many factors that make maths a difficult subject, there are many others that make it easy to learn. The first is that babies are born mathematical – human brains created or identified mathematics, and there are aspects of human development that make maths easy for us, such as music and an appreciation of beauty and pattern. Finally, what makes it easy to understand maths is when it connects to the everyday maths that is an inevitable part of real life.

Born mathematical

Numerous studies (outlined in, for example, Pound 2006a) indicate that certainly within the first year of life (and in some studies within the first days of life) babies can:

▶ differentiate between different numbers of objects visually or aurally. This usually occurs with very small numbers, say two or three, and may involve looking at dots on a card, jumps made by puppets, or listening to words with different numbers of syllables. In some studies where moving objects were shown on a screen, babies were able to detect changes in larger numbers. There are claims (Doman and Doman 1994) that babies as young as three months can be taught to recognise and discriminate between both groups of dots and numerals up to 100. This is not without controversy, based both on the quality of research involved and the morality of spending extensive periods of time with such young infants on this one aspect of human development.

▶ make connections between a number of sounds heard and a number of objects seen. When hearing, for example, two drumbeats, babies will look at a set of two rather than three objects.

▶ recognise and register surprise when objects are added to or taken away from a group of, say, two objects and do not result in the correct number being visible.

▶ demonstrate an ability to discriminate between two-dimensional shapes such as triangles, squares and circles.

▶ show interest in tasks that require problem-solving, concentrating hard to achieve some desired end such as reaching a toy but quickly losing interest if the problem is too simple.

▶ begin to categorise objects and to investigate cause and effect. Seven-month-old Charlie was playing with a small collection of toys and everyday objects. Among the varied treasures in his basket was a small felt ball and a wooden ball of a similar size.

He spent a long time apparently attempting to put one ball and then the other into his mouth. The word *apparently* is used because the observer assumed that he was actually using his mouth, as the most sensitive area of the body, to gauge the size and textures of the balls. After a while, he took one ball in each hand and shook them. The wooden ball rattled but the felt ball did not. He switched hands and tried again, repeating this exercise three times before putting the balls aside and beginning to explore some of the other objects. Interestingly, when he returned to the basket later in the day, he repeated this sequence of activities.

▶ seek out and enjoy patterns. Patterns are a fundamental aspect of mathematics (and a feature of human thinking in general) and will be considered more fully in Chapter 4.

Using songs and rhymes

Another factor that makes it easy for children to develop mathematically is the use of songs and rhymes. One of the universal functions of music is to make things easy to remember (Pound and Harrison 2003). In everyday lives throughout the world, human beings use music to support memory. The strong link between music and memory may be seen in:

▶ advertisers wanting us to remember which toothpaste or soft drink to buy;
▶ recalling a special event when we hear a special song or piece of music;
▶ commercial audiotapes designed to help children learn tables;
▶ folk songs and ballads that commemorate events in history or legend.

Practitioners in the early years make good use of this function of music. Every single practitioner probably knows and uses dozens of counting songs and rhymes, most of which have finger actions to accompany them. The complex business of memorising number names in the right order (an ability without which counting is meaningless) is made easier by:

▶ the use of tunes and/or rhythms that support memory.
▶ the inclusion of finger actions that stimulate the brain in remembering number names. The part of the brain responsible

7

for counting is next to the part of the brain that is responsible for controlling fingers. Stimulating one part thus stimulates the other.

▶ group involvement, which means that children enjoy the social aspects of music-making, another important function of music.

Helen MacGregor (1998) has written a number of songs, all of which are set to familiar tunes, about many other aspects of mathematics (in addition to counting). Her three songs about circles, squares and triangles, catchy and happily sung by young children, also have hand actions and thus are also highly memorable.

Irresistible attraction

Mathematics has a beauty or intrinsic interest that has been called 'the poetry of mathematics' (Pound 2006a, citing Thoreau and Einstein). The widespread use of the term *numeracy* when talking about mathematical development has led many people to think only about the functional aspects of maths. What instils interest and enthusiasm in this area of development for some children may not be about what you can *do* with maths but a fascination with numbers and quantities, or pattern and size. Papert, one of the pioneers of using computers for mathematics with young children, describes his own childhood passion for cogs and ratios, after visiting a mill (Pound 2006a). Similarly, Devi, who has been described as a human computer, talks about falling in love with numbers and seeing them as toys. As an adult she determined that she would show others that maths was not boring but beautiful (Devi 1990).

Three-year-old Isabel, for example, loves to play with circles. She has a set of nesting circular cardboard boxes with lids that she enjoys stacking, nesting lids and boxes separately. She sometimes begins with the smallest and sometimes with the largest. She draws concentric circles on every piece of paper she can find. Four-year-old Mike loves big numbers; sometimes he writes numbers with lots of zeroes at the end and sometimes taps out similar numbers on a calculator. In both cases he regularly checks with adults, asking what the numbers say.

Making it real

Whatever practitioners do to support young children's mathematical development, including problem-solving and reasoning, will never have as much effect as the active involvement of parents in their children's learning and development. Research over two decades has highlighted the huge importance of parents' interest and involvement in general and more specifically in relation to mathematical thinking and understanding. It follows, therefore, that making maths easier relies heavily on getting parents involved and making maths more relevant to children's everyday lives. This vital aspect of supporting children's mathematical development will be explored more fully in Chapter 10.

The notion of basing mathematical thinking and development on what is real for children will be a constant theme throughout this book. If you think back to your own childhood, the memories of mathematical teaching and learning that you hold probably seem to have little or no connection to what you knew of the real world. It is generally agreed that this is one of the reasons that maths is perceived as difficult. Sarah, training to be a teacher, offers an excellent example of what happens when maths appears to lack relevance. In a maths session at university, the group of which she was a member were cutting out squared paper to represent hundreds, tens and units. Suddenly, she exclaimed, as she saw ten strips of ten squares fitting neatly into a hundred square, that she had never realised what she was doing when she was doing sums involving hundreds, tens and units. Although she had successfully undertaken maths GCSE, Sarah had done little more than she was told, simply following the steps without ever reflecting on what the process she was undertaking really meant. The importance of promoting thinking about mathematics will be returned to throughout this book.

Sarah did not find maths easy but because she wanted to be a teacher she persevered and achieved her goal. However, it was only in the process of training to become a teacher that she grew to understand and enjoy thinking mathematically. Practitioners working with young children will find it more effective to begin by enabling young children to like mathematics. It is possible to teach some young children to do abstract calculations, but unless children experience a combination of understanding and enjoyment they are unlikely to remain motivated and engaged. Early years practitioners have an awesome responsibility. What happens in the early years supports or undermines future development. If in the process of sitting on the rug reciting numbers or sitting at a table doing tedious worksheets, children learn that maths and numbers are boring – that will have to be unlearnt before they can progress properly.

An example of this comes from the ability of young children, mentioned earlier in this chapter, to recognise small groups of objects. This is known

9

as subitising and it appears that although present in babies it is rarely acknowledged in early years settings and schools. Children who in their early years are willing to guess correctly that they have seen five, six or even seven objects without having had the opportunity to actually count them, by the age of five are often unwilling to guess (Pound 2006a). This may be in part because children at this stage of development are:

▶ reaching an age when they wish to avoid making mistakes (Pound and Harrison 2003);
▶ going through a period when they like to count everything in sight (Gardner 1993);
▶ often obsessed with repetition, so they enjoy repeating stories, songs and number names long after adults have ceased to enjoy the activity. This claim can be substantiated by any practitioner or parent who has had to read the same story or sing the same song over and over and over again.

However, it is also likely that the children's reluctance to estimate (or subitise) may be because adults are most likely to respond to children's estimates of quantity, whether right or wrong, by saying 'let's count'. How many times have you asked children how many apples or pencils or dolls you are holding and then ignored their responses, whether right or wrong, and begun to count the objects out loud? Of course, practitioners' motives are good ones. We all want children to learn to recite the number names in the correct order but it would sometimes be possible, whether children's responses are accurate or not, to respond by saying things such as:

▶ I think you're right – let's see. Yes there are three because there's one for you, one for Sam and one for me.
▶ Seven? Pretty close – I think there might be six. How can we find out if there are enough?
▶ What makes you think there are five?

The point of going into so much detail about subitising is that it seems likely that adults' failure to respond to these guesses is connected to some children's later difficulties in calculation (Butterworth 2005). Some children of nursery age were found to be able to identify groups of six or seven objects (Macnamara 1996). However, later when they were in the reception class the same children were generally found to be unwilling to even try to identify the number without actually counting them. The few children who did persevere were often able to identify even larger groups. One, for example, when asked how he knew there were eleven objects responded by saying that he had seen seven and counted four more.

HARD OR EASY?

What is interesting about the research on subitising is that one of the common difficulties faced by children at Key Stage 1 (or even Key Stage 2) is the business of counting on. Older children, asked to add fifteen and seven, might be seen to be counting out fifteen and then seven more, rather than holding the large number in their heads and counting on seven. Yet in this study some children of four or five years of age appeared to be able to do that spontaneously. It has been suggested that it is what adults do that supports or gets in the way of continuity in learning (Butterworth 2005). Steffe (2004) believes that adults must first find out what young children can do and make that the basis of their teaching, a view that owes much to the writings and philosophy of Piaget and Vygotsky. He contrasts this with the all too common approach that consists of 'transferring the teacher's mathematical knowledge from the head of the teacher to the heads of children by means of the words of the language' (Steffe 2004: 235).

Since mathematics appears to be a natural or innate ability then we must teach it in a way that takes account of what children already know. There will be some important differences if we set out to teach children in this way: what Steffe terms 'the mathematics of children' (2004: 235). This is because their experiences will be very different. Practitioners cannot find out about the mathematics of children simply by asking, since children themselves often do not know, or do not know what is relevant. A clear view of children's thinking about and understanding of mathematics can only be found out through:

▶ *Genuine listening and sustained shared conversation.* Simply asking questions, even open-ended questions, does not give real insight into learning or understanding.
▶ *Detailed observation of and engagement in children's extended imaginative play and practical, meaningful and relevant experiences.* When the things that children are engaged in really matter to them, adults can observe not only what they genuinely know and can do but also what matters to them.

11

KEY POINTS

The abstract nature of mathematics and concern for accuracy make maths a hard subject. However, the fact that humans are born mathematical makes it very much easier to learn than it would otherwise be. The use of songs and rhymes supports mathematical learning, but even more important in supporting mathematical thinking and learning is an approach that seeks to:

- ▶ understand the nature of mathematical thinking and learning;
- ▶ find out what children already know and can do;
- ▶ give children opportunities to explore and thus demonstrate what motivates or interests them.

Chapter 2

There's more to maths than numbers

> ▶ Babies' and children's mathematical development occurs as they seek patterns, make connections and recognise relationships through finding out about and working with numbers and counting, with sorting and matching and with shape, space and measures.
> ▶ Children use their knowledge and skills in these areas to solve problems, generate new questions and make connections across other areas of learning and development.
>
> (DfES 2007: 61)

In this chapter you will:

▶ explore what is involved in the curriculum for Problem-solving, Reasoning and Numeracy (PSRN);

▶ consider the things that children have to understand and learn in order to be able to think mathematically, including an understanding of pattern, estimating and abstract thought;

▶ review the complex nature of some of the aspects of mathematical development, such as counting, that are widely considered to be simple.

Practitioners working with young children tend to focus almost exclusively on number. This means that the full breadth of the curriculum identified in the EYFS is often under-represented in practice. The guidance for PSRN requires practitioners to address goals for:

▶ numbers and labels and for counting
▶ calculating
▶ shape, space and measures.

13

However, these three large categories encompass a vast array of skills, knowledge and understanding, essential to mathematical understanding, thinking and development. The knowledge involved in shape, space and measures involves, for example, two- and three-dimensional shape, pattern, symmetry, position, time, length, height, weight, capacity. A simple analysis of the descriptions of development in PSRN (DfES 2007) includes:

▶ **Actions**, such as responding, noticing changes, developing awareness, recognising, matching, comparing, counting out, investigating, representing, selecting, classifying, organising, observing, categorising, separating, sharing, finding out, attempting, ordering, sorting, creating, and presenting results.

▶ **Thinking processes**, such as logic, distinguishing between different characteristics, being alert to, and understanding variations, identifying similarities and differences, and investigating things that challenge expectations.

▶ **Talking**, such as using relevant vocabulary and number names and positional language, describing solutions.

▶ **Dispositions for learning**, such as enjoyment, showing curiosity and interest, and being alert.

These four categories overlap with one another. In order to describe how you arrived at a solution or answer to someone else you will probably talk, but you will also be thinking. Similarly, if you are enjoying something you are likely to be engaged in a range of actions that might include sorting, selecting and comparing. There is, of course, an overlap between the six areas of learning and development. For example, in the guidance for calculating (DfES 2007: 67) it states in the section dealing with babies under a year of age that babies 'are logical thinkers from birth'. This contributes to their later ability to calculate – but it also contributes to the development of language and their ability to make sense of the world in general – which will involve science, technology and so on.

The other important factor to remember is that young children are learning more than one thing at a time. This means that developing mathematical language does not always have to be addressed in a wholly mathematical context. The adults' main focus in a particular cooking group may be on motor skills such as learning to use tools, but that will not prevent them from using mathematical language such as number names and comparative language such as *larger*, *smaller* and so on.

THE COMPLEXITY OF NUMBER

Each aspect of mathematical development is complex. The references to development contained in EYFS underline the broad and complex range of behaviours that come together to support mathematical development. Simply in order to count, children have to be able to understand that:

▶ Number names must be said in the same order every time they are used (known as the stable order principle). This is of course why adults spend such a lot of time helping children to remember number names in order.

▶ Each item in a group must only be counted once and must only have one number name applied to it (known as the one-to-one principle). Young children often have difficulty with this – sometimes because they simply rush to recite all the number names they know and sometimes because they apparently have decided how many there are in a group and just reel off the words without ensuring that they match words and objects one-to-one.

▶ The last counting word or number name that is said when counting a group of objects tells you how many are in a group (known as the cardinal principle). This, of course, only works if the number names are said in the right order.

▶ Counting can be applied to anything, things that are similar or things that are different or things that do not even exist (known as the abstraction principle).

▶ Items in a group can be counted in any order. As long as one-to-one, stable order, cardinal and abstraction principles are applied the same number will be found every time.

So every time we ask children to count something they are using at least some of these principles, and in order to count accurately will need to move towards using them all simultaneously – quite a tall order. However, at the same time they have to become aware of the many different ways and contexts in which we use number words. Just the simple word *five* might mean:

▶ exactly five as in five fingers or five eggs;
▶ approximately five as in five minutes;
▶ five years on a birthday;

15

▶ twenty-five minutes on an analogue clock or watch;

▶ fifth as in the car we are pointing at when we have counted five in a row. But it might also mean house number 5, or, if the street is numbered with odd numbers on one side and even on the other, house number 9 or 10;

▶ five metres, litres, centimetres, grammes, etc. This is particularly puzzling because five might be any of these very different things: 500 grammes printed on a bottle or tube does not match up to any five things that can be readily held or seen. If placed on digital scales the reading will probably not include a 5 because the weight of the container will be included in the reading, rather than the weight of the contents.

In addition to these different mathematical and everyday uses of number words children must also contend with the fact that:

▶ Numbers may have no mathematical meaning – a number 5 bus is not bigger than a number 4 bus, nor does it necessarily arrive after it. PIN numbers, phone numbers, etc. have no mathematical significance.

▶ Written numbers can be written in a variety of ways without changing their meaning, such as *five*, 5 and *V*. The numeral 5 looks very like S and is easily confused with 3. Two separate symbols systems, counting and writing, are used almost interchangeably.

THE REAL FOUNDATIONS OF MATHEMATICAL DEVELOPMENT

This is clearly a very wide range of aspects of learning, all of which have to be developed and supported. Action, thought, talk and dispositions are inextricably linked to one another. In addition, in this chapter, four 'real foundations' or cornerstones of mathematics – pattern-seeking, estimating, problem-finding and solving, and the development of abstract thought – will be considered.

Pattern-seeking

The curriculum guidance (QCA 2000) that preceded EYFS placed little emphasis on pattern. Yet pattern is of fundamental importance not only

 16

in mathematical thinking but in thinking in general. Human beings are born pattern-seekers – we come into the world looking for the pattern of other human faces. And this interest in patterns remains with us throughout life, helping us to make sense of the world, to predict what might happen next. Mathematics has been called 'the science of patterns' (Devlin 2000) since mathematicians are constantly seeking new patterns to explain and predict aspects of mathematics.

The development of children's understanding of pattern seems not to be clearly understood. It is described differently by different authors. This vital aspect of mathematics will be explored in greater detail in Chapter 4. Pattern-seeking is closely related to the other aspects identified in EYFS defined at the beginning of this chapter. It involves making connections and identifying relationships, similarities and differences in considering number, categorisation, shape, space and measures. It is one element of problem-solving and it is certainly cross-curricular.

Keep them guessing

As suggested in Chapter 1, mathematics involves a great deal of estimation. It may be referred to as predicting, approximating or hypothesising. I have chosen to refer to it as guessing because guessing is something young children understand quite well. Guessing also links well to intuition – two terms that many people balk at in relation to maths, but in fact they have much to contribute to the development of mathematical thinking:

▶ Not all mathematical thinking relies on logic and reason. Adults should encourage children to use the full range of their thinking abilities, which includes guessing, estimating, predicting or hypothesising.

▶ 'Mathematical discovery (includes) trial and error, guesswork, intuition and conversation with others' (Pound 2006a: 67, citing Devlin).

▶ Intuition is the basis of new ideas and involves 'expertise, judgement, attentiveness and reflection on experience' (ibid: 67, citing Claxton).

▶ Practitioners need to help children to know something 'in their bones'. 'Once they have an intuitive understanding of and feel for mathematics, they can then move on to understand it at a more abstract, generalized objective level' (Schiro 2004: 57).

17

▶ Guessing helps to ensure that sensible answers are achieved. When using a calculator, for example, it is all too easy to come up with a wildly inaccurate answer by simply pressing the wrong key or by being unclear where the decimal point should go. Guessing beforehand gives a ball park figure that might just lead you to check an answer that doesn't seem right.

▶ Children's guesses give adults a window on their thinking. Some people prefer to talk about 'informed guessing' but in fact all guesses are informed. Children's guesses are rarely, if ever, random. They are informed by the knowledge and understanding that children currently have. What adults think of as a 'wild' guess is usually an indication that children do not understand what is being asked of them. If you ask a child what shape something is and they reply 'yellow', you will have a clear indication that they do not understand what you are asking. Similarly, if you ask children to guess 'how many' and a child guesses thirty-nine when there are in fact six, you might assume that they think there are a lot and that they may not be confident about how many six actually is. Guesses may be playful but this is an indication that children are beginning to try to abstract and generalise their ideas.

Problem-finding/problem-solving

Human beings appear driven to find and solve problems. Adults like murder mysteries, sudokus, crossword puzzles, riddles – things both large and trivial that we feel driven to work at until we solve them. This is even true of babies and toddlers who often drive themselves to master new skills and abilities, and then having succeeded immediately make the task more challenging – and simply begin again. Soon after learning to walk, Xav spent extended periods of time pushing a small wooden trolley over different surfaces in different areas of the garden. Grass, gravel, slopes, manhole covers – all presented a challenge and he would keep returning to a particular one until he seemed satisfied. He also challenged himself by pushing heavy loads (such as blocks) or awkward items (such as a large watering can) in his trolley.

Problem-solving is a core element of mathematical thinking. This is reflected in EYFS where problem-solving is identified as the first of the three aspects of the maths curriculum. But problem-solving requires children to be resourceful, creative, persistent and confident. Perhaps above all it requires that children feel secure enough to risk getting something wrong. It also relies on experience. The experiences on which children draw in order to solve mathematical problems are not always primarily mathematical. In imaginative group play, for example, children will be learning to decide, to imagine, to predict, to plan and to reason as they negotiate the narrative of their game with other children. These are all skills involved in problem-solving. Similarly, in block play, the problems that present themselves as children build give them insight into doubles, halves and quarters; length and weight, symmetry and sequence. These insights can in turn be used to support subsequent problem-solving, particularly if adults help children to make connections between the different areas and aspects of learning.

The importance of motivation or interest in problem-solving should not be under-estimated. The mathematical problems that are presented to children have to be exciting – in a way that the problems so often associated with school maths are quite definitely not. When you were at school, did you really care how long it took three men to dig a hole of a certain size or fill a hypothetical bath? What practitioners should be aiming for is for children not simply to be problem-solving but problem-finding with all the exuberance and enthusiasm with which they found and tackled problems in infancy. Problem-finding involves being curious – wanting to know – and this is what adults supporting mathematical development should be seeking to foster.

In a lively book entitled *Counting on Frank* (Clement 1995), a young boy shows enormous curiosity in imagining how tall he would be if he grew at the same rate as a tree in the garden, or how high the toast would pop up if the toaster were as big as a house, and in calculating how many cans of dog food it would take to fill the shopping bag. In the end he wins a trip to Hawaii because he has a very accurate idea of how many sweets are in a jar – he has had so much practice at estimating. This boy is a problem-finder with all the curiosity and excitement practitioners should be trying to develop in all the children with whom they work.

Learning to think in the abstract

It has been suggested that mathematics is the most abstract subject of all (Devlin 2000). Practitioners are well aware of its abstract nature and for this reason try to make all aspects of the subject as accessible as possible by using concrete materials, real situations and practical contexts to support mathematical development. This is, of course, essential, but unfortunately it is not enough. In order to support the development of the abstract thought that is essential to mathematical thinking and learning, practitioners must focus specifically on processes that will promote this kind of thinking. This will involve:

▶ **Communication**, which includes not only talk but also gesture, facial expression and body language. It promotes thinking because when children communicate with others they are coming to understand what other people are thinking.

▶ **Symbolisation**, which might be in the form of writing, drawing or other forms of representation. Fingers are very commonly used by young children as mathematical symbols, for example when they hold up two or three fingers to represent how many cars they have or all ten of their fingers to symbolise a lot. Mark-making and drawing also allow children to develop understanding as they represent their ideas (Worthington and Carruthers 2003).

▶ **Visualisation**, or thinking about things that cannot be seen. All the games we play with young children that include hiding things in bags or boxes or the use of feely bags promote visualisation. This encourages children to think about things that are not visible – an essential element of abstract thinking.

▶ **Imagination**, which involves thinking about things that are not present. Many mathematicians have become interested in imagination because they see it as part of a staged development towards learning to think in the abstract. Devlin (2000) suggests that there are four stages – the first of which is thinking about real things in the immediate environment but perhaps having a different function or being placed elsewhere. The second stage that Devlin suggests is the stage at which monkeys and apes operate and it involves thinking about real things that cannot at the time be sensed or perceived for example through smell or touch. The third level of abstract thought comes into play once language is used. This supports thinking about things that may never have been seen or even previously imagined. Finally, Devlin suggests that the level at which mathematical abstract thinking occurs involves being able to think about things that do not exist in the real world. These ideas will be developed further in the chapters that follow.

KEY POINTS

There is much more to mathematics than number, calculation, shape, space and measures. Each of these areas is in itself complex and involves a great deal of conceptual development. Wide-ranging and extensive real-life, practical and meaningful experiences are needed to ensure that children are enabled to build firm foundations for learning about mathematics. Building such foundations will also involve learning to:

▶ guess or estimate
▶ think in the abstract
▶ identify patterns and
▶ find and solve problems.

Chapter 3

Maths is about life

Mathematics is not about number but about life.

(Devlin 2000: 76)

In this chapter you will:

► consider some opportunities for supporting mathematical development in everyday experiences and activities;

► review the importance of helping children to make connections;

► explore the importance of developing opportunities for mathematical development in children's imaginative play; and

► think about ways of identifying children's key enthusiasms and using them to promote mathematical development.

In Chapters 1 and 2, the rationale for approaching children's mathematical development in innovative ways has been explored. In this chapter the focus is on making maths 'real' for children. An important part of making things real for children of course depends on helping them to make connections between maths in the real world, their everyday experiences and maths that happens in the school or early years setting. However, part of what is real for children is their play, so this too will be examined and some opportunities for promoting mathematical development explored. Above all, what is real for young children are the things that they are fascinated by, that they are interested in or even passionate about. It is these things that make the best starting points for mathematical (and other) learning.

TABLE 3.1 Examples of the ways in which mathematical thinking and learning can be developed in everyday and routine situations, both at home and in group settings

Aspect of PSRN	Home-based everyday maths	Setting-based everyday maths
Number	From the moment children get up to the time they go to bed everyday life offers hundreds of opportunities for seeing and hearing numbers – clocks, washing machines, cookers, mealtimes, phone books, newspapers, etc.	Opportunities include asking children how many pieces of fruit or paintbrushes will be needed. Adults can also draw children's attention to displays and books that include numerals.
▲ guessing	Adults can encourage guessing in all sorts of everyday contexts simply by beginning with 'I wonder how many . . .'. Encouraging children to wonder, for example, how many apples or blocks might fit in a particular bag or box increases interest and helps to prevent children worrying about getting something wrong, since the answer can always begin with 'It could be . . .'. It is similarly helpful to include some examples for which there is no certain answer such as 'I wonder how many elephants could fit in this bus'.	
▲ pattern	Maps, phone directories, bus or train timetables and take-away menus often include a pattern of numbers that interest children.	Daily routines such as counting how many children are absent, or how many will sit at each table for lunch encourage children to identify number patterns.
▲ problem-finding	Modelling finding and solving number-problems that occur in everyday life helps children to develop strategies of their own. For example, when putting together a shopping list, adults might say things such as 'I'm not sure how many eggs I've got – I'd better count them. I wonder if that will be enough.' The adult might similarly count chairs or pieces of fruit. Checking cutlery for lunch provides a useful potential problem, since two or three items are required for each person.	
▲ abstract thought	Abstract thinking about number can be promoted by asking children to think about numbers of things that cannot readily be seen. Asking, for example, whether all the bikes are out requires children to think about how many there usually are and checking that against what they can see – quite a sophisticated process. In thinking about how many food items, such as apples, will be needed for a family or other group, children will need to think about members of the group that they cannot see – a parent may be at work, an older brother or sister at school.	

■ TABLE 3.1 *continued*

Aspect of PSRN	Home-based everyday maths	Setting-based everyday maths
Calculating	Opportunities for calculating will be similar to those for developing understanding of number. The difference often lies in asking slightly different questions. 'How many ...?' needs to be supplemented with questions such as 'How many more ...?' or 'Who has more ...?' or 'How many more (or less) ... do I need?'.	
▲ guessing	We saw in Chapter 1 that it is important to encourage children to guess or estimate before (or sometimes even instead of) counting. This is equally true for calculation. Getting into the habit of coming up with an approximate answer promotes the idea of checking and thus guarding against illogical answers. It has the added benefit of enabling adults to assess children's understanding.	
▲ pattern	Children can be helped to see the patterns in calculations by adults remarking on them. Egg boxes and bun tins provide excellent material for comments that raise children's awareness of number patterns, such as 'That's funny, yesterday we had four eggs and two spaces but today we have two eggs and four spaces'.	
▲ problem-finding	The same kinds of contexts that offer opportunities for counting also support problem-finding and problem-solving in relation to calculation. Indeed, sometimes the age, experience and confidence of children will mean that similar problems will be solved in different ways. Alternatively, children can be encouraged to calculate not just whether there are enough knives, forks and spoons but how many more or less will be needed.	
▲ abstract thought	Montague-Smith (2002) reminds us that asking children of three and four years of age to describe how they know that their calculation is correct is often met with silence. We can encourage abstract thought and thinking in general by demonstrating what we mean. Simply by saying things such as 'I knew we had two tins of beans in the cupboard and now we've got two more – so we must have four altogether', adults encourage children to explore the ideas presented. This might be reinforced by holding up four fingers to act as symbols for the tins.	
	It is also important, by the way, to ask questions like this whether children's answers appear right or wrong. Their reasoning will often surprise you. Giving explanations should not come to be associated only with getting it wrong.	
Shape, space and measures	Everyday conversations at home include innumerable spontaneous references to relative size, to position and to measures. Sorting out the washing gives opportunities to talk about bigger, smaller, nearly as big as, etc. Talking while cleaning or putting away	It is important in early years settings to replicate and extend these everyday opportunities to develop children's understanding of shape, space and measures. In addition staff will need to plan both for opportunities that meet the general needs of children and of individuals. In one setting, for example, the focus was on length.

shopping will include phrases such as on top of, beside, underneath. Putting petrol in the car, buying fruit or choosing carpet provide rich opportunities for developing understanding of these important areas of mathematics.

▲ guessing

Simply playing with the relevant language can be easily done and very effective in supporting mathematical learning. 'I just can't remember where I put that new toy. Is it on top of the fridge? Is it in the cupboard? Is it underneath the bed?'.

▲ pattern

Maintaining the pattern of the day is helpful in encouraging children to develop understanding of time, sequence and pattern.

▲ problem-finding

Wrapping parcels provides plenty of opportunities for talking and learning about shape, space and measures. 'Which piece of paper is the best shape for this present?' 'Will I have enough ribbon to tie up this package?' 'Put this piece of Sellotape here on top but we will need another to go underneath'.

▲ abstract thought

Creating hypothetical situations concerning shape, space and measures is a good way to promote abstract thought. Depending on the age of children, at group times adults might extend a story by asking children what would have happened if. . . . 'What if . . .?' questions are an excellent way of getting children to think about things that are not present. Even simple things like checking with children whether you have everything you need for a walk in the park encourages them to envisage things and situations that are not visible.

Children were given a range of natural materials that encouraged them to compare length, and staff planned to incorporate relevant vocabulary such as longer, shorter, etc. One child enjoyed playing with ropes in the outdoor area. With him in mind, staff provided some coils of rope, some curly gift ribbons and some elastic. A group of children became very interested in this collection and used it to guess how far pieces would reach, which was the longest when stretched or the shortest.

The activity described above is an excellent one for promoting guessing as it is often difficult to tell which length of rope or ribbon or elastic will stretch the furthest.

Providing pictures or other examples, such as fabric of different kinds of pattern, and incorporating relevant vocabulary (see Chapter 4) when talking about them will support understanding of pattern.

The same length activity becomes a problem-solving one if you encourage children to find the best piece of string for tying a parcel or the most suitable length of rope for pulling a truck.

EVERYDAY MATHS

Opportunities drawn from everyday life to develop mathematical thinking and understanding are immense. Since, as we have seen, maths is part of everything we do, that is inevitable. Indeed, around the world, most curricula for young children do not have a strand or component that is called mathematics or numeracy, but that is not to say that children do not develop these understandings. In Scotland, in the foundation stage, mathematics has been subsumed under Knowledge and Understanding of the World, since maths is regarded as just another way of understanding the world around us.

The opportunities offered might be about everyday life in the home such as cooking, shopping, washing, decorating, cleaning, ordering a take-away, celebrating birthdays and other family events, going on holiday or watching television. All of these everyday events have scope to support children's mathematical understanding and experience. Similarly, in early years settings, the everyday life of the group offers rich opportunities. These may include the day-to-day routines particular to group settings such as the arrangements for snacks or other small group times. There will, however, be some of the same opportunities that exist in the home. This is especially important for children experiencing day care, who must also have opportunities to cook, hang out washing and ride on buses.

Table 3.1 identifies some of the opportunities offered by everyday activities at home and in the early years setting for mathematical thinking and learning.

IMAGINED WORLDS

Imaginative play will be explored in more detail in Chapter 5, but it would not be possible to explore what is real for children without mentioning the world of their imagination. Gura (1992) reminds us that we should not think of play as simply a means to a learning end. Real play allows children to explore their interests and adults need to tread carefully. We ought not to hijack children's intentions in order to address only the learning intentions we have selected. This can all too easily destroy the play and erode children's enthusiasm. As was suggested in Chapter 1 we should be looking for children's mathematics and making that our starting point. It is very tempting to approach a child at the sand tray and seize the opportunity to ask how many cups of sand will be needed to fill the bucket. How often has a child faced with such questions either stood silently waiting for the adult to go away again or moved on to play elsewhere?

Play allows children to:

▶ **Make sense of the world.** In their play children explore the world, including the mathematical world. Home corner play for example allows children to explore the mathematical concepts involved in cooking, in developing the sequences of events involved in routines such as getting ready for school or going to bed and getting up again. Playing at shops enables children to explore the complicated exchanges that occur in shopping transactions. These can look very confusing to young children – the shopper asks for goods, gives the shopkeeper a piece of paper and receives goods and lots of money (small change) in return.

▶ **Interact socially**, learning from other people's ideas – those of both children and adults. This may occur in conversation or through observation of how others go about things. Imitation is sometimes thought of as a low-level activity but developmental psychology (see for example Nadel and Butterworth 1999) has increasingly been able to demonstrate the value of imitation to learning. Although adults have, of course, an important role to play in providing good models for imitation, interestingly, it appears that other children provide even better models. So although adults may demonstrate counting and calculating and explore shapes and patterns with children, they will learn more from each other. There is no substitute for the time and space in which to play with and learn from peers.

▶ **Practise new learning.** This might be as simple as children writing 4 over and over again whenever they get the chance or as complicated as children undertaking what Gura (1992) refers to as 'stunt building' with wooden blocks. Children's intentions are not primarily mathematical but these complicated structures offer many opportunities to explore and learn about comparative sizes, positional language, weight and balance. The importance of playful practice is that children engage in it for much longer and with more engagement than they would do for something that is imposed by others. If we tried to get babies to practise walking for the long hours that they spend when mastering the skill, we would find it very difficult indeed. But the fact that their practice is self-imposed means that they spend hours and hours, falling over, getting up, falling over, getting up – only made more determined by their failures.

27

Compare this to the reluctant child asked to complete a worksheet in order to practise writing numbers or adding groups – easily discouraged or distracted, looking and feeling tired.

PASSIONATE ABOUT LEARNING

For babies, of course, what Athey (2007) terms their *persistent concerns* are the only possible starting point for learning. As they grow older they remain the most effective basis for teaching. Children's enthusiasms, or even obsessions, should not normally be regarded as a barrier to learning but a vital component in supporting and extending learning. In order to learn effectively, children need to be excited and enthusiastic. When this happens the chemistry of the brain changes, making the brain more receptive to learning. A note should be added about children with special educational needs. Opinions vary as to whether children with autistic spectrum disorder should be encouraged to pursue their obsessions, but overall it appears that, as with other children, they form a good starting point.

Careful analysis of their observations of children can help adults to understand what they are interested in. This can sometimes bring surprises. The child who looks as though he or she is wandering aimlessly may in fact be seeking out opportunities to follow a preferred schema (Athey 2007) or way of exploring space. James, for example, loved to position things, so he would move from area to area lining up cars; carefully placing blocks all around the edge of the table; creating patterns of shells around the edge of the sandtray and so on. This interest offered many opportunities for mathematical thinking and learning and staff targeted him for particular vocabulary connected with pattern, sequences and length. They also ensured that a range of activities included materials that would support his interest.

One group of three- and four-year-old children were very interested in minibeasts, searching the garden for specimens and studying books to increase their knowledge. Their teacher brought in a copy of *Snail Trail* by Ruth Brown (2000) and the children became very enthusiastic about the snail's journey – taking photographs of each other hanging *upside down* like the snail, or going *through* a tunnel, or *under* a bridge. They wrote a song to the tune of *London Bridge is Falling Down* that incorporated a host of positional language and which they rehearsed over and over again – singing it as they created snail trails in the workshop area or described roadways and train tracks.

Sometimes, play that is not focused on mathematical concepts can be made richer in supporting mathematical thinking and learning by adding resources that capture children's imagination. Adding numbers to wheeled toys in the garden and numbered parking bays can spark a lot of talk about numbers. Adding a real clock and an appointment book and pencils to the hospital play highlights some mathematical ideas and encourages children to explore (or play about with) mathematical concepts. Adding socks of different sizes and patterns to the home corner can have a similar effect. This can be even more stimulating if teddy is there too, with one sock missing.

MAKING CONNECTIONS

It is important to remember that learning occurs when children can make connections. Linking new aspects of learning to something they already know fosters interest and understanding. Those connections may be between:

▶ Real events involving mathematics that happen when children are at home (or out and about) with their families and what happens in the early years settings – such as going shopping with mum and going shopping in a group with other children and members of staff.

▶ The mathematics that occurs in play and that is reinforced in story or other group activities – such as imaginary space travel that includes talk of weightlessness and unthinkable distances, which may be followed up with a board game about astronauts and further stimulated by reading and exploring *Man on the Moon* (Bartram 2002).

▶ A child's preferred schema or interest and pictures and resources that mirror that schema or interest, allowing children to explore the connections. Four-year-old Zac's interest in big things, for example, caused him to make connections between dinosaurs and construction machinery. Seeing a double bass for the first time his comment was that if a diplodocus sat on it, it would break. He made the connections that helped him to think about things that mattered to him, but at the same time he was exploring the important mathematical concepts of relative size.

It is important to ensure that some of the connections we help children to make are unexpected or challenge the connections that have been

29

made, because that is where learning occurs. Large but light parcels in the post-office area alongside heavy but very small packages are an example of how we may do this. A tiny bag containing a very long silk scarf or a container that looks as though it should contain one thing but in fact contains something quite different help children to talk about and therefore to reconsider connections and learning.

What adults do can also act as a barrier to children trying to make connections. EYFS (DfES 2007: 4.3) reminds practitioners that making connections is vital to critical and creative thinking and suggest that 'it is difficult for children to make creative connections in learning when colouring in a worksheet'.

KEY POINTS

If it is to be successful, mathematical thinking and learning must be real for children. It may be made real or meaningful by drawing on or connecting with their everyday experiences. It may feel real or relevant because it is incorporated into and connected with their imaginative play. Above all, it will be real for them if they see connections between what adults want them to learn and what they themselves are interested in. Learning occurs wherever connections are made or challenged by unexpected connections.

Chapter 4

Looking for patterns

> Mathematics is the science of order. Here, I mean order in the sense of pattern and regularity. It is the goal of mathematics to identify and describe sources of order, kinds of order, and the relations between the various kinds of order that occur.
>
> (Devlin 2000: 73, citing Gleason)

In this chapter you will:

▶ consider what is meant by pattern and where it exists;
▶ identify some important vocabulary used to define pattern;
▶ examine some ways in which adults can help children to describe and create patterns.

It has been said that 'the brain thrives on patterns' (Lucas 2001: 18). This is because we identify patterns wherever we can in order to make sense of the world. Where we cannot find a pattern we create a best-fit pattern, a set of rules or an ordering process that makes events manageable. We are born pattern-seekers, emerging from the womb at birth looking for patterns in faces. Having identified faces at birth, babies will imitate what they see – they will smile in response to a smile, poke out their tongues in response to seeing someone else do that. At birth, babies begin to make social contact and it is their interest in the pattern that makes up the human face that drives that contact. This interest continues throughout life but we remain good at recognising faces, which we do through a speedy process of pattern-recognition.

WHAT IS PATTERN?

Young children often call their drawings or paintings a pattern when they are not intended to represent anything in particular. If they have not set out to draw a person or a dog, for example, they may say that they have made a pattern. However, even adults find it surprisingly difficult to describe pattern. This may be because although we think of patterns as a particular arrangement – probably involving a particular sequence, perhaps symmetrical, perhaps cyclical – not all patterns follow these rules precisely. Indeed, many patterns do not involve exact sequences but can still be described as patterns. The pattern on a zebra skin, for example, is not regular or symmetrical but it is a pattern. Devlin (2000: 72, citing Sawyer) explains this as follows:

> 'Mathematics is the classification and study of all possible patterns.' Pattern is here used . . . to cover almost any kind of regularity that can be recognized by the mind.

WHY IS PATTERN IMPORTANT IN MATHEMATICS?

Pattern in everyday life is most often associated with clothing, fabrics and wallpapers but of course there is a pattern to the day, patterns in nature, patterns in behaviour or actions, as well as in stories and songs. Understanding pattern helps children to understand regularity, to notice the impact of rules, and to make generalisations. These understandings will eventually pave the way for understanding algebra, but before that they will help children to apply rules. As the authors of *Starting Out* (BEAM 2003: 82) remind us:

> To be able to repeat a sequence pattern of blocks of colour, or of shapes, numbers, sounds or movements, children must identify the implicit rule in the sequence . . . To make growing patterns, you decide on the unit and you have to apply the same rule again and again to form an increasing or decreasing sequence. When singing and enacting *Five little ducks went swimming one day*, for example, you have to remember the unit 'one little duck' and the rule 'take away' each time the rhyme comes round again.

SUPPORTING AWARENESS AND UNDERSTANDING OF PATTERN

Although mathematics has been called 'the science of pattern', this has not always been evident in the mathematics curriculum. The *Curriculum Guidance for the Foundation Stage* (QCA 2000: 80), for example, had but one short phrase that mentioned pattern, namely 'talk about, recognise and recreate simple patterns'. Although this remains a learning goal in EYFS (DfES 2007: 72) within early years practice in the section entitled 'Planning and Resourcing', practitioners are now advised that they should:

> Provide materials and resources for children to observe and describe patterns in the indoor and outdoor environment and in daily routines, orally, in pictures or using objects.

This may include patterns in rhymes and songs, number squares and the patterns that children themselves create in art, music and dance. The pictures referred to may include illustrations from books, postcards and photographs. Although an improvement on previous guidance, given how fundamental to mathematics pattern is, this does not go far enough. There is, for example, little mention of music or poetry, both of which rely heavily on pattern. Indeed, if mathematics is the science of pattern, music and dance must be the arts of pattern. We need to explore ways of encouraging children to think about pattern not just visually and orally as the guidance suggests, but through movement and listening as well.

Almost everything that is written about young children's understanding and creation of pattern is based on what they know about visual pattern. Table 4.1, which illustrates different authors' views of the development of children's understanding of pattern, shows a clear bias towards the visual.

However, not all patterns are visual. As pointed out in *Starting Out* (BEAM 2003) music, songs, dances and stories all include patterns. What these descriptions of the development of pattern in young children show or tell the reader is that there is no clear cut, single process of development and that different children will develop in different ways.

The key to identifying and describing pattern with young children may lie in identifying the vocabulary with which they can describe pattern and making efforts to apply that vocabulary to children's mark-making, musical improvisations, dance or action sequences or work with materials

33

TABLE 4.1 Descriptions of the development of pattern in young children

Adapted from Montague-Smith (2002: 69)	Adapted from Early Childhood Mathematics Group (1997: 10–11)		Adapted from BEAM Education (2003: 83)
Describe an order	Describe a pattern	Intuitively makes spatial patterns	Seemingly random arrangements of marks etc. referring to finished product as a pattern
Describe and make line patterns	Copy it and extend it	Recognises, copies, extends and creates patterns which become more complex with experience	'Splodge patterns' with paint and folded paper, similarities identified
Copy a sequence	Make a more complex pattern than the previous one	Discuss their patterns with an increasing range of vocabulary	Simple repeating patterns using beads
Create a sequence	Make or continue a sequence pattern that goes in more than one direction	Progressing from simple alternating patterns to sequences of repeated patterns	Able to continue a pattern started by someone else
Create a pattern	Recognise, extend and create a growth pattern	Sequences of repeated patterns in more than one direction (symmetrical, radial or surrounding)	Discusses a repeated pattern and identifies a feature of it
Recognise cyclic patterns	Make and explain simple symmetrical patterns	Making growth patterns (e.g. staircases)	Able to make or copy a growing or decreasing pattern
		Moving on from splodge patterns to symmetry by folding and cutting	

such as shells or stones. The words that adults might plan to draw into conversations with children about pattern might include:

- ▶ sequences
- ▶ repeating patterns
- ▶ symmetrical patterns
- ▶ growing patterns
- ▶ increasing patterns
- ▶ decreasing patterns
- ▶ reverse order
- ▶ alternating patterns
- ▶ cyclical patterns
- ▶ surrounding pattern
- ▶ radial patterns
- ▶ staircase patterns.

Case Study 1

The staff of an early years setting felt that they could do more to develop children's understanding of pattern, so they made it a focus of their planning. They checked their resources and identified everything that they thought could be used to support pattern making. They found a number of things that they thought would be useful, including:

▶ large wooden blocks

▶ small wooden blocks

▶ coloured plastic shapes

▶ musical instruments and sound makers

▶ threading beads

▶ counting toys

▶ a basket of shells

▶ pattern blocks, to which they added unbreakable mirrors (some non-slip mats were also added, which enabled children to place the blocks without becoming too frustrated).

They decided to supplement these items with some more natural materials and were able to source and buy some dried seed heads, dried leaves of different shapes and sizes and some black and white pebbles. One member of staff had a large collection of buttons and brought these in, which brought back happy childhood memories for a number of staff. Another had seen some clothes pegs in a local chain store and everyone felt that these would be a good resource for pattern-making. In fact, most members of staff had some pegs to spare and before long they had an enormous collection of large, small, plastic, wooden, coloured and plain pegs.

They noticed that the EYFS advice (DfES 2007: 71) suggested collecting pictures 'that illustrate the use of shapes and patterns from a variety of cultures' and between them they found they had some suitable pictures. They managed to find some particularly beautiful cards from the Early Excellence Training and Resource Centre in Huddersfield. They also saw at the interactive centre at Early Excellence some postcards illustrating natural patterns such as tree rings and spiders' webs. These were placed alongside small trays of coloured sand in which children could trace out the patterns. They decided to laminate two sets of cards so that children could talk to one another about the cards or could play memory or matching games, as well as buying some small trays and coloured sand.

One member of staff remembered that some years ago they had used some socks to explore pairs and size. They dug them out of the cupboard and found that there were some with interesting patterns, which they supplemented by visiting local pound shops and markets buying several additional pairs ranging from man-size football socks to dolls' tiny ones. They found some rhymes about socks and put these onto laminated cards.

The staff also identified some songs and stories that had strong patterns in their structure, and these included:

▶ traditional stories such as 'Goldilocks and the Three Bears' and the 'Billy Goats Gruff';

▶ songs with obvious patterns such as 'Old MacDonald had a Farm';

▶ some counting books with strong patterns such as *One is a Snail and Ten is a Crab* (Sayre and Sayre 2004) or *Ten Terrible Dinosaurs* (Stickland 1997);

▶ some story books with strong patterns such as *Bear Hunt* (Rosen and Oxenbury 1993).

They also identified some books that are *about* pattern such as:

▶ *Aliens love Underpants* (Freedman and Cort 2007);

▶ *Pants* (Andreae and Sharratt 2007).

They found two music books by Helen MacGregor and Bobbie Gargrave particularly helpful:

▶ *Let's go Shoolie-shoo* (2004); and

▶ *Let's go Zudie-o* (2001).

These both include a CD and although *Let's go Shoolie-shoo* is aimed at children from five to seven years of age it does have some interesting pieces of music for exploring pattern. *Let's go Zudie-o* is aimed at children from three to five years of age and staff particularly enjoyed the fact that it includes suggestions for cross-curricular work. They resolved to make sure that every class did some musical pattern-making.

PATTERN ACROSS THE CURRICULUM

Although the focus of this book is mathematics, pattern is firmly embedded in our everyday lives and if we are to help children to make the connections that will support learning it is essential that we approach it in a cross-curricular fashion. Since pattern is so fundamental to all aspects of mathematical development it is vital that it is given a much stronger focus than is currently the case. Enhancing children's understanding and awareness of pattern in stories, art and music will give them more material with which to understand pattern in mathematics. Table 4.2 identifies some ways in which pattern can be developed across the curriculum.

The routines that children experience are themselves patterns and contribute not only to their personal, social and emotional development but to their mathematical understanding as well. The pattern of days, weeks and years are part of children's growing understanding of the world. Helping them to understand the way in which time and sequences have a pattern and can therefore be predicted gives shape and meaning to what can otherwise seem like random events.

TABLE 4.2 Developing pattern across the curriculum

Area of learning	Examples of activities that support understanding of pattern
Creative development	▶ 2- and 3-D art activities ▶ use of interesting materials for collage and 'play' with mirrors and OHP ▶ identifying pattern in nature and in found materials ▶ creating patterns in small world play ▶ creating patterns in role play, e.g. shop ▶ singing ▶ playing musical instruments ▶ using instruments and/or body sounds to represent visual patterns ▶ using visual materials such as stones, pegs, shells to represent aural patterns
Personal, social and emotional development	▶ circle time ▶ taking turns ▶ routines
Communication, language and literacy	▶ poetry and rhymes ▶ graphic patterns ▶ stories with repeating patterns ▶ describing and talking about patterns, using relevant vocabulary
Problem-solving, reasoning and numeracy	▶ number squares ▶ investigations and problem-solving ▶ pattern blocks ▶ block construction involving a pattern
Knowledge and understanding of the world	▶ art software ▶ music software ▶ days of the week ▶ seasons of the year ▶ growing ▶ cooking ▶ construction sets and blocks ▶ exploring natural materials
Physical development	▶ patterns of movement – dance and/or use of apparatus ▶ clapping games ▶ patterns made from body sounds, e.g. stamping, tapping, etc.

KEY POINTS

Pattern is of fundamental importance in children's growing understanding of mathematics. It is important that practitioners feel able to describe and identify pattern in order to support children's growing awareness. Pattern may be identified and created physically, visually and through listening. It is also important that children are encouraged to explore pattern not simply in relation to mathematics but in every area of learning and development. Genuine understanding requires rich and varied experiences.

Chapter 5

Playing maths

The child's preoccupation with fantasy and imagination is vital to development.

(Jenkinson 2001: 79, citing Pearce)

In this chapter you will:

▶ consider the importance of play and playfulness in thinking mathematically and learning mathematics;

▶ explore some of the ways in which children can learn to find and solve problems in their play;

▶ examine the differences between child-initiated learning and adult-directed but playful teaching.

THE IMPORTANCE OF PLAY AND PLAYFULNESS

Although we encourage playfulness and creativity in most other aspects of young children's development we rarely do so in relation to mathematics. We certainly don't readily make jokes about maths, and yet humour and fun are vital elements of young children's learning. As adults, we revel in children's playful teasing and clowning. If they suggest that there is a lion under the table we engage with the idea — asking what we should do. Should we offer the lion some food (as happens in *The Tiger who Came to Tea* by Judith Kerr, 2006)? Should we be very quiet, or perhaps make a loud noise in the hope of frightening the lion away? We enter into the fun.

If, however, children suggest that they have 49 cars, when we know that they have six or seven, adults' immediate reaction is to suggest that we count them to check – we do not like jokes about numbers. Some of this reluctance to allow playfulness in relation to mathematics springs from the methods that have traditionally been used to teach the subject in schools – with an emphasis on facts and accuracy. This is not to say that accurate answers do not have a place but that accuracy is only important in some contexts. If I want to get to the moon, I'd better be very accurate and if I'm sharing sweets with a sibling I'll need to make sure that I get a fair share – which might mean that I should get more! Context is vital and so often we expect children to rehearse and practise mathematical ideas without any real purpose. Making it real (as discussed in Chapter 3) makes all the difference.

Adults' unwillingness to joke or be playful about mathematics can also be connected to their own lack of confidence. This may in part have arisen because they were not encouraged or allowed to play around with mathematical ideas and concepts when they were children. In the same way as playing with construction materials helps the learner to know them better and therefore to use them more effectively, so playing about with the complex ideas and concepts associated with mathematics can help the learner to use them more confidently and effectively.

Play is an essential element of all learning – but particularly of young children's learning. There are many theories about why this should be the case. The consensus of opinion seems to be that playing about with ideas that are not real can enable children to think more clearly about what is real (Meek 1985). In relation to mathematics, play has the added importance of promoting the abstract thought essential to the subject as well as supporting mathematical development in general.

PLAYFUL LEARNING

There are a number of ways in which practitioners can make mathematical experience and learning more playful. The following sections will focus on:

1   child-initiated experiences;
2   the use of books, stories, songs and rhymes;
3   encouraging guessing and promoting playful, imaginative ideas and conversation.

Child-initiated experiences

Child-initiated action is perhaps the one essential element of play and as such is common to most definitions of play. Most books and materials on supporting mathematical thinking and learning emphasise adult-directed activities but practitioners must not lose sight of the fact that if play is important to learning it is important to all learning, including mathematics (or PSRN). A form of organisation sometimes called continuous provision, which enables children to take responsibility for managing time and accessing resources, supports child-initiated activity. Children are able to initiate learning activities and experiences that meet their needs and interests. This may mean that children spend long periods of time in one area of provision or it may mean that they move between different areas, reinforcing their own learning through the use of different materials and resources.

For example, Josh liked to spend long periods of time in the outdoor area, where he particularly loved the wheeled toys. One member of the staff team worried that since Josh spent so much time outside he was not accessing the whole curriculum. In order to address her anxiety it was decided that team members would observe his play and discuss among themselves whether or not he was learning and thinking about mathematics. Table 5.1 highlights the learning that staff observed and what it taught them both about Josh's mathematical development and the impact of play decisions.

Julie, on the other hand, appeared to flit from area to area. Members of staff were equally worried about her – feeling that she did not concentrate or focus well on learning opportunities. Similar observations of her suggested that, far from not concentrating, Julie demonstrated a strong commitment to particular ideas and interests – as Table 5.2 indicates. The table also suggests ways in which play and PSRN opportunities can be extended.

Every area of continuous provision, indoors and out, can be used to extend mathematical thinking and learning, as the examples shown in Table 5.3 indicate.

The use of books, stories, songs and rhymes

EYFS endorses the importance of the use of stories, songs and rhymes (DfES 2007: 62). All three, like play itself, make a major contribution to children's (and adults') understanding of what might otherwise be isolated events or occurrences. We use stories to make sense of the world

TABLE 5.1 Demonstrating the development of child-initiated mathematical thinking and learning in one area of provision

Aspect of PSRN	Observation	Comment
Number		General comment: there were many observations of Josh riding bikes and trucks. Spatial awareness has an impact on a range of cognitive abilities including understanding of number.
▲ guessing	Adult: How many firefighters' helmets have we got today? J.: I think there are four.	J. is willing to estimate how many helmets there are – and his guess is correct.
▲ pattern	J. spends a great deal of time creating parking bays, using large planks. He says each one needs three planks, which he sets out in an orderly and regular fashion.	
▲ problem-finding	J. tries to fit four things (tyre, plank, ball and helmet) onto a truck in a variety of ways – moving the truck after each attempt to check whether any fall off.	The group have listened to and enjoyed *How will we get to the beach?* (Luciani and Tharlet 2003) in which a mother tries to get five things, including her baby, to the beach. Her car beaks down, the bus driver won't let her take the turtle on to the bus, the ball won't fit on the bike and so on. Eventually they find transport and spend the day on the beach.
▲ abstract thought	J. (talking to two other boys): Pretend you're two tigers.	This use of imagination is a step towards abstract thinking (see Chapter 2).
Calculating		
▲ guessing	J.: I don't think there are enough bikes for me and my friends. Two people will have to wait.	J. demonstrates that he can calculate the difference between the number in the group of friends and the number of bikes.

TABLE 5.1 *continued*

Aspect of PSRN	Observation	Comment
▲ pattern	Referring to the planks he is using for parking bays, J. comments: I've got ten planks but I can't use them all because I need three for each bay – I haven't got enough to make another parking bay.	These observations suggest that J. is well on his way to achieving goals for calculating.
▲ problem-finding	J. continues: I think I need two more. Yes two more planks.	
▲ abstract thought	Holding up ten fingers, J. explains to adult: I had ten planks and I made three parking bays – see? (bunching fingers together in threes). So now I've got one left and I need two more.	J.'s fingers act as symbols. This demonstrates that he is moving towards understanding that one thing can stand for another – a vital concept in developing mathematical thinking and learning.
Shape, space and measures		
▲ guessing	J. is able to steer a path between a number of different obstacles very accurately.	J.'s experience of steering wheeled toys of different kinds means that he is very confident about estimating whether or not a particular vehicle will be able to get through a particular space.
▲ pattern	J. sets out tyres and planks to create a course for trucks and bikes. In doing this he creates a symmetrical pattern.	
▲ problem-finding	In addition J. looks for the longest piece of hosepipe.	J. went about finding the longest piece of hose very systematically laying out each piece in turn and starting at the same place.
▲ abstract thought	At the end of the session one of the staff team asked J. to describe the roadway he had built. With her help he drew it on the flipchart.	Representing his ideas on paper gives further evidence that J. is developing the abstract thinking necessary to mathematical thinking and learning.

TABLE 5.2 Extending child-initiated mathematical thinking and learning across different areas of provision

Aspect of PSRN	Observation	What next?
Number	General comment: At the time of these observations, Julie had recently moved house. The observations were largely recorded when she was playing with the dolls' house, at the dough table and in the sand tray. She also spent considerable periods of time pushing a doll's pram – into which she would gather and dispense different resources and materials as she passed different areas – a block, a tambourine, a book, etc.	
▲ guessing	J. (talking to doll): I think you've got three toys – oh no only two.	Much of J.'s time is taken up with imaginative play – re-enacting domestic scenes in the dolls' house, playing birthday parties in the dough and sand. Imagination is vital to the abstract thought required in mathematics.
▲ pattern	At the dough table J. has placed 'cakes' in each of the six spaces in a bun tin. She places three sticks in each of the cakes on one side of the tin – and two candles in the remaining cakes. She explains: I'm three and Jodie is two. 333,222; 232323.	J.'s play and mathematical understanding could be extended by adding to this area cutters of different sizes; bun tins or similar trays with different numbers and patterns of spaces; and plates of different sizes.
▲ problem-finding	J. looks for a plate big enough for all her cakes. Finds two small ones and shares out the cakes – carrying them to the home corner and placing them on the table there.	It could be further extended by moving the dough table into the home corner and setting up different numbers of plates and chairs.

Aspect of PSRN	Observation	What next?
▲ abstract thought	The birthday cakes (described above) spark an extended period of imaginative play – blowing out candles, singing 'happy birthday' and sharing out cakes. The candles and cakes are representations enabling her to act out her experiences in her imaginative play.	Alternatively children could make, bake and decorate a variety of pretend cakes for use in the home corner – with a variety of bun tins, plates and cake tins in which to place them.
Calculating		
▲ guessing	Filling a bucket at the sand tray, J. says: I'm going to need two more scoops of sand – oh no I need another one – that makes three.	Adults plan to place some additional materials near the sand tray to encourage J.'s interest in pattern-making – some pebbles, twigs, etc. One member of staff finds some pictures on the Internet of castles and decorated sandcastles and copies of these are added to the area.
▲ pattern	Putting shells on her sandcastles, J. says: 4, 4, 4, 4. I've done two on this one – now I need two more to get to four.	They also think that adding some small-world play figures will extend play opportunities and involvement but want to observe further to see which aspect will be more productive. Play people on the beach or princesses in castles are both possibilities.
▲ problem-finding	J. is sharing out paper flags between her sandcastles – she puts one flag in each, and then begins to put another one in each – stopping when she realises that she hasn't got enough. An adult suggests that she makes some more flags and she does this with straws and masking tape until each sandcastle has two flags.	

J.: I'm going to need three more flags and then all the castles will have two flags. (This conversation shows that she is beginning to visualise.)

Shape, space and measures

▲ guessing

That baby (pointing to a large teddy) is too big for my buggy.

▲ pattern

Sets up cones in a line and zig-zags between them with the pram.

▲ problem-finding

J. tries the teddy in a pram but because of all the things she has already placed in there the teddy topples off. She then takes everything out of the pram places the teddy in first and begins to replace everything else, wedging things around the teddy. This process continues for some time until she is confident that everything is more stable.

▲ abstract thought

The play that follows involves J. in replacing the objects in the pram in a variety of locations around the garden. This process is part of an elaborate game of taking teddy to different houses and visiting people.

Staff decide to add some more large-scale construction materials – ropes, crates, tyres, etc. – to develop the play that is emerging. They see mathematical potential in the roadway, fitting things inside containers and developing spatial awareness in which J. seems to be engrossed.

TABLE 5.3 Showing examples of opportunities for extending mathematical thinking and learning in areas of continuous provision

Area of provision	Indoor examples	Outdoor examples
Role play	Resources provided should always include relevant items to stimulate mathematical thinking and learning about time and measurement. A hospital corner for example could include: ▲ clock ▲ appointment book ▲ squared paper for temperature chart ▲ calendar ▲ tape measure ▲ scales.	Large-scale materials to promote creative and imaginative role play with a mathematical bias might include: ▲ helmets ▲ hose pipe ▲ traffic cones ▲ planks, tyres, crates, etc. ▲ large bags and boxes ▲ rope, lengths of chain.
Small-world play	In addition to the normal range of small-world play materials, sets of small-world play materials to explore stories with a particular mathematical content stimulate mathematical play and exploration. *Handa's Surprise* (Browne 1995), for example, offers lots of opportunities for counting and calculation.	Small-word play outdoors might also involve symbolic use of natural materials such as: ▲ cones ▲ stones ▲ twigs ▲ shells. By simply adding a large basket to these resources, children might be encouraged to re-present *Handa's Surprise* (Browne 1995).
Natural, malleable and tactile materials	Offering natural materials such as stones and twigs in the sand area may promote pattern-making.	Long lengths of drainpipe and large containers of different sizes allow children to explore shape, space and measures.

Creative Workshop	A large box filled with many more boxes, again filled with more and more boxes attracts children for whom containing is a particular interest. It also offers an excellent opportunity for learning more about shape, space and measures.	A huge box (such as the box for a washing machine) may be filled with crates which in turn contain other smaller boxes or blocks. This offers a large-scale mirroring of indoor provision.
Construction	Construction materials of all sorts support understanding of pattern, and many aspects of shape, space and measures. Unit blocks also offer insights into halves, quarters, doubles, etc.	Large construction using drainpipes, tyres, etc. supports pattern-making, shape, space and measures.
Mark-making materials	Adding materials such as raffle tickets and diaries to the drawing and writing area can stimulate an interest in maths.	Large-scale mark-making materials such as markers and playground chalk, together with tape measures, stop watches, clipboards and note books can lead to mathematical explorations.
		Whiteboards left with skittle games might encourage children to keep scores or tallies.
		Squeezy bottles of paint on snow (or water on tarmac) allow children to explore trajectories – the height and distance that the liquid can be squirted.
Books	Books should be found throughout the setting as well as in the book corner. Adding books on pattern to the block area, for example, can stimulate new kinds of play with blocks.	A small collection of books made available outdoors might include reference books on diggers – to promote conversations about size, weight, strength, etc. There might also be story books such as The Treasure Hunt (Butterworth 2003) that might develop an interest in problem-solving.
Resources for science	Making magnifying glasses readily available (indoors and out) promotes discussion of size, pattern, etc. A collection of science resources that children can readily find supports mathematical and scientific understanding.	A growing area and a wildlife area make children aware of time and the pattern of the seasons.

TABLE 5.3 *continued*

Area of provision	Indoor examples	Outdoor examples
ICT	Beebots (or Roamers or Pixies) are excellent resources for encouraging estimation, counting, judging distance, etc.	Children could be encouraged to use a digital camera to find examples of patterns, numbers, particular shapes, etc. in the environment – either the garden or the neighbourhood.
Music and sound-making materials	In Chapter 8 the close link between music and maths will be considered.	Opportunities for music-making outdoors enable children to explore loud sounds. Lengths of drainpipe cut to different lengths and played with a flip-flop or table tennis bat promote discussion of comparative length (and how it changes the sound).
Physical play	Children up to the age of three should have indoor opportunities for climbing, etc. as this promotes spatial awareness and confidence. Hollow blocks require physical effort and develop understanding of weight, ratio, etc.	A range of small apparatus, such as balls, hoops, etc. appropriate to the age of the children supports spatial awareness. Opportunities for gross motor activity provide a firm foundation for many aspects of mathematical development. The development of mathematical vocabulary of 'inside', 'above', etc. is supported by physical action.
Quiet areas	Quiet areas or dens provide children with an understanding of enclosed space – they can also support paired or small group, sustained shared thinking vital to mathematical thinking (see Chapter 6).	
Open spaces	Open spaces can be difficult to achieve indoors, but being flexible so that sometimes large spaces can be offered for block play or roadways on train tracks can give children the opportunity to explore large spaces and boundaries – contributing to mathematical understanding.	Open spaces outside might include a large space for running as well as a roadway for vehicles. These activities can enhance spatial awareness, and understanding of shape, space and measures.
Materials for exploring and categorising and containers	Materials and containers should be selected on the basis of the age of the children who will be using them and where they are going to be used. For babies it might be collections of heuristic play materials, whereas for older children collections of shells, stones, glass pebbles, socks, balls and so on. Such collections offer opportunities for comparing, categorising and so on.	
	A variety of containers again need to be selected on the basis of the age of the children, where they are going to be used and the nature of the materials. They might include, empty boxes (large or small), bags, trucks, baskets, etc. Moving things from one place to another – or from one container to another – appears to support children's understanding of a number of mathematical concepts. It also provides experiences that may contribute to problem-solving.	

– to explore possibilities in both the real and imagined worlds. All practitioners are familiar with traditional stories such as the 'Three Bears' or the 'Three Billy-goats Gruff', but since mathematics is one way of describing the world around us, there are literally hundreds of stories that explore mathematical concepts.

Mick Inkpen's *The Blue Balloon* (2006) explores shape and size – pages, or parts of pages, folding out to demonstrate the changing dimensions of the balloon. There is an imaginative element in that the balloon lifts the boy high into the air – but does deliver him home again in time for tea. *Shoe Baby* (Dunbar and Dunbar 2005) on the other hand explores relative size through fantasy. A giant baby travels over land, sea and air in his father's shoe – prompting lots of discussion about what size a giant might be if his shoe were the size of a car.

Shrinking Sam (Latimer 2007) and *One Too Many Tigers* (Cowell and Ellis 2001) are good examples of the way in which story can address both mathematical concepts and the emotions that underpin and shape all human thinking and behaviour. In both books, the underlying element is sibling rivalry. Sam shrinks as his parents appear to favour his big brother and baby sister. The illustrations show the impact of his decreasing size – peas the size of footballs, falling down the drain and so on. In *One Too Many Tigers* the mathematics is readily apparent but the emotional undercurrent concerns the young tiger's unwillingness to find room for the new baby on the family's tree.

These story elements make the ideas memorable, which is also what songs and rhymes do. As discussed in Chapter 1, everyone finds it easier to commit to memory lists or facts when words are set to music or given both the rhythm and rhyme of poetry, particularly when finger actions are added (Ramachandran and Blakeslee 1999). Every early years practitioner probably knows hundreds of counting songs and rhymes and these support children in learning number names in the right order. Children generally enjoy joining in with these number songs and rhymes. In addition there are a number of books that use known tunes to develop counting songs. *Over in the Grasslands* (Wilson and Bartlett 2002), for example, uses the form and structure of the song 'Down in the Jungle where Nobody Goes' to create a counting book featuring a mother rhinoceros and 1 baby; a mother hippopotamus and 2 babies, a mother eagle and 3 baby eagles and so on.

Songs and rhymes can be made even more attractive to children by creating songs tailored to their specific interests. This can be very easily done by setting the words of an existing counting book to a known

51

tune. *Ten Terrible Dinosaurs* (Stickland 1997), for example, works very well to the tune of *Ten green bottles*. Alternatively a known song can be used to fit in with the mathematical interests of a particular child or group of children. This need not be confined to counting songs. The story of *Who Sank the Boat?* (Allen 1988), which is essentially about problem-solving, can be retold through words set to the tune of 'Here we go Round the Mulberry Bush'. The words that appear in the text fit quite well but if you like you can just reduce it to a series of verses reflecting the story, beginning with:

Was it the cow who sank the boat, sank the boat, sank the boat?
Was it the cow who sank the boat
On a warm and sunny morning?

Encouraging guessing

The encouragement of guessing and the promotion of playful, imaginative ideas and conversation will be dealt with more fully in the next two chapters. However, it is important to remember that talk and imagination enable children to make mathematical sense of the world around them. When children discuss ideas and interact with others in imaginative play they are learning to deal with other people's ideas and to think about things that may not be visible. This in turn supports the development of concepts and abstract thought.

Although much of play consists of exploration, at least as much involves imagination. These two elements of play together enable children to know and understand the materials or situations in which they are engaged in different ways. Moyles (1989) has described the process by which this occurs as a play spiral. Pinder, riding her new bike around the garden, alternated between:

▶ the physical exploration of her own strength and the spatial layout of the garden; and
▶ imaginative play in which she and any available adults became customers at a garage or mechanics fixing the bike.

This play sequence involved mathematical thinking and learning about:

▶ dispositions for learning (confidence and perseverance);
▶ the development of spatial awareness;

- ▶ measurement – such as: How far did she cycle? How long did it take her?;
- ▶ closely observing the cogs on the bike and comparing their sizes;
- ▶ the vocabulary associated with the price of repairs, how long it would need to stay at the garage, cause and effect.

PLAYFUL TEACHING

This phrase has been used by a number of writers but is often associated in this country with the work of Janet Moyles (Moyles and Adams 2001). Unfortunately, some practitioners assume that any activity or experience that is not formal (such as a worksheet) is play. This is not the case. Many of the activities that practitioners offer children as play are in fact playful teaching. This can be very helpful if targeted to support or scaffold children's current understanding but it does not replace the need for genuine open-ended play in which children initiate and explore their own learning. Teaching that is not playful, interesting or stimulating will be counter-productive.

The staff team in an early years unit set up a skittle game in the outdoor area. Some children began to play there, developing as they played some rules about what should happen to the skittles that had been knocked down. A further group of older children were directed to the same area. They had been instructed to find a way of keeping the score so that they could discuss it with an adult later in the session. The first group were initiating their own activity – the second were engaged in a playful task set by the teacher.

Maths games are often used as part of a playful teaching approach. If they are always played on adults' terms they will not make room for learning – or what was referred to in Chapter 1 as 'the mathematics of children' (Steffe 2004). Lesley Hill (Marsden and Woodbridge 2005: 24) describes setting up a new maths area in her reception classroom. She had provided blank games boards and used as counters penguins and polar bears, which linked to their theme. Although the first session had been successful, Lesley Hill writes:

> I cautiously planned the second game. I hoped I could offer a challenge that would excite and engage the children as well as teaching them new skills. Would I be prepared to let them take the lead and change the game if they wanted? Would I try and steer it back to my objectives?

53

Would I be prepared to abandon my objectives if the children weren't interested? I decided to make the game as playful as I could, as well as being prepared to include their own ideas and connect them into my game where I was able. I was however going to stick to my objectives although I had worked out several strategies to get them where I needed them.

To Hill's surprise, the children began the session by raising the issues that had been her objective – to introduce the idea of following rules. Their comments included the following:

▶ We need rules so we know what the game's like and what you can do in games.
▶ We need to check that all the people are not being naughty like moving too much or going the wrong way.
▶ You mustn't move yours too many to win.
▶ I know that it's different rules for different games.

Hill (in Marsden and Woodbridge 2005: 24) concludes by commenting 'throughout the project I was surprised how often the children came up with what I had planned or even went beyond it.' Playful teaching demands that early years practitioners plan carefully on the basis of what they know about children. They must also be willing to be flexible, reacting to the way in which children approach the activities and experiences that have been offered.

KEY POINTS

This chapter has emphasised the role of imagination, play and fantasy in mathematical thinking and learning. Playful teaching is of great value if it promotes playful learning. Activities regarded by adults as playful will only support learning if children are able to connect or engage with the planned teaching.

Chapter 6

Thinking maths

> We are moving towards a different way of teaching [maths] . . . that is not just concerned with kids' conceptual knowledge but with the quality of their underlying thinking.
>
> (Barnard, cited in Pound 2006a: 153)

In this chapter you will:

▶ consider the ways in which thinking develops in young children;
▶ explore some of the ways in which problem-solving and reasoning as well as abstract thinking can be supported;
▶ look at the role of thinking about thinking in young children's development.

Children's thinking is both complex and fascinating. Fisher (1995) suggests that education has sometimes worked against the development of thinking by promoting the idea that learning involves simply being told. He gives the example of a child saying 'I think in the playground when I go out to play' (Fisher 1995: ix). The idea of an empty brain, passively waiting for thoughts to be delivered does not match with current neuroscientific knowledge. Nor is it in line with the effective practice required in the foundation stage (DfES 2007: 4.3), which highlights the importance of making connections and of sustained shared thinking.

These two aspects of thinking serve to remind practitioners that thinking is not a private activity, arising out of a vacuum – but a social and cultural activity that depends on other people (Rogoff 2003). This view of young children's thinking and learning has important implications for practitioners since it demands that adults are reflective and aware of their own thought processes.

55

Not least among those implications is the importance of developing the sustained shared thinking that is described in EYFS (DfES 2007) as involving:

▶ The adult being aware of the children's interests and understandings and the adult and children working together to develop an idea or skill. . . .

▶ Responsive, trusting relationships between adults and children.

▶ The adult in showing a genuine interest, offering encouragement, clarifying ideas and asking open questions. This supports and extends the children's thinking and helps children to make connections in learning.

(based on DfES 2007: 4.3)

We must also remember that children's thinking is not only supported by adults but by 'all the other thinking children' (Marsden and Woodbridge 2005: 79) with whom they come into contact. Sustained shared thinking need not only happen between children and adults, it can also occur within small groups of children.

EYFS (DfES 2007: 67) suggests that children are 'logical thinkers from birth', a view supported by Gopnik *et al.* (1999). Claxton (1997), on the other hand, argues that it is possible to think too much and that we should not lose sight of unconscious processes, such as intuition. Children's common answer to a question 'I just knowed' is an example of this. This should not deter adults from asking the question. Over time children will engage with this idea and begin to offer explanations.

So thinking may be logical – but it may not be. It may involve reasoning but may also involve some guesses or hunches. Piaget studied children's logic (Inhelder and Piaget 1958) and was surprised that young children's answer to the question 'Where does the wind come from?' was that the wind came from the fact that the trees were waving about. Young children are logical but their experience and knowledge are limited, which means that they do not always come to the right conclusion but their thinking should be respected.

Thinking may be creative or reflective, imaginative, convergent, divergent, scientific, visual, mimetic or somatic. In fact, there are probably as many attempts to define types of thinking as there are people writing about them. This chapter will focus on problem-solving and reasoning because they are highlighted in EYFS in the title of this area of learning and development. It will also explore abstract thought, since it is so vital to children's later progress in mathematics. In conclusion there will be some consideration of the role of metacognition or thinking about thinking, in young children's mathematical development.

THE ROOTS OF THINKING

However types of thinking are categorised there will inevitably be some overlap. There are, for example, many ways of thinking logically – some of which may sometimes be said to be illogical if the starting points are not sound (or are not shared by you). Reasoning may or may not be logical – and logic may or may not be reasonable. We cannot know in what ways or how a baby thinks since they can't tell us, yet we can often make assumptions about their thinking from the way in which they act. Neuroscience tells us (for example, Eliot 1999: 334), however, that 'experience rewires the brain'. That is why rich and real mathematical experiences are of such great importance.

The learning and experiences that fill infancy are largely physical. This early physical (or somatic) learning is the foundation from which all subsequent learning and thinking develop. There is widespread agreement among theorists (Piaget 1952; Bruner 1986; Gardner 1993; Athey 2007) that long before children are able to think in the abstract their thinking is rooted in physical action – sometimes called enactive or sensorimotor thinking. At a later stage thinking rests on objects and words that can represent or stand for the object or idea. Max, for example, not yet two years of age, tries to match representations with another – if, for example, he sees a penguin on TV, then he looks for his plastic penguin (Karmiloff-Smith, cited in Pound 2006a: 7). This would be termed by Bruner (1986) as iconic thought. Over time, children begin to move into symbolic representation or thinking using story, dramatic play, movement, models, images and sounds (both verbal and musical). These in turn develop into representations that use symbol systems such as writing and numerals.

There are both similarities and differences between the way in which adults and children think. Even adults may use enactive and iconic modes of thought when dealing with something new or complex – you have only to watch a group of adults settling a joint restaurant bill to know this. Everyone puts into the kitty what they've been told by someone else is the right amount but, without doubt, the money will be sorted and re-sorted into piles as everyone struggles to come up with the right answer through enactive modes of thinking.

The greatest difference between children's and adults' thinking comes from the fact that children have less experience. Claxton (1997) reminds us that although children are more likely than adults to use physical action, imagination, intuition, dreams and feelings in their thinking, this does not mean that these are invalid or childish ways of thinking. He suggests that they should indeed be seen as the foundation of children's future learning.

Fisher (1995: 19) highlights the importance of sensory thought, in particular what he terms visual thinking. He suggests that 'spatial imagery is the prime source of thought' and emphasises visual thinking. Other writers highlight the importance of other sensory input into thinking. For Healy (1999: 219) the experience of 'building intelligent muscles', or knowing with the body, is vital to thought. Clements (1998: 3), writing more specifically about mathematics, underlines the value of physical action:

> children's ideas about shape do not come from passive looking . . . they come as children's bodies, hands, eyes . . . and minds . . . engage in action . . . Merely seeing and naming pictures is insufficient. . . . They have to explore the parts and attributes of shapes.

He goes on to suggest that this needs to be done in a number of ways – drawing, moving, folding, manipulating, creating shapes – in order to ensure that the concepts involved have been fully explored and understood. This means that play with materials that require spatial awareness – blocks, bikes, fitting objects into boxes and so on – is vital to understanding. In turn, this means that young children need a wide range of active experiences in order to lay the foundations for the thinking they will need to develop as they become mathematicians. Fisher (1995) points out that thinking based on the senses (in particular what he terms visual thinking) is the key to problem-solving. (Adults must of course ensure that children without good sight are not disadvantaged but that they make full use of their sensory abilities.)

PROBLEM-SOLVING AND REASONING

Logic is the form of thinking most commonly associated with mathematics. However, mathematics requires much more than logic, which is just one of many approaches (Gardner 1993; Devlin 2000) needed to support mathematical thinking. As EYFS (DfES 2007) points out, mathematical understanding involves problem-solving and reasoning, which in turn involve:

- ▶ classifying;
- ▶ symbolic representation;
- ▶ categorisation;
- ▶ comparing;
- ▶ working through a problem;
- ▶ noticing patterns;
- ▶ logic;
- ▶ distinguishing between different characteristics;
- ▶ understanding variations;
- ▶ identifying similarities and differences; and
- ▶ investigating things that challenge expectations.

(based on DfES 2007)

Perhaps the most important attribute in becoming a problem-solver is to be a problem-finder (Pound 2006a). Babies are born problem-finders. From birth humans are driven to create new challenges for themselves. Posing formal or irrelevant mathematical problems too soon can rob young children of the enthusiasm that was discussed in Chapter 2 as being vital to successful problem-finding/problem-solving.

In Chapter 2 it was stated that problem-solving requires resourcefulness, creativity, persistence and confidence. Adults need to encourage children to use a range of strategies. Some strategies such as trial and error or acting on a hunch seem to come naturally. But we can promote creative and imaginative ideas by modelling them or by encouraging children to try them out. It's important that children come to know that making mistakes (even in mathematics) is not only all right but is a positive step in learning. As Fisher (1995) reminds us, the only way to have good ideas is to have lots of ideas – and that means that thinking will include a number of less than good ideas which children will need to explore. Adults cannot do children's thinking for them.

The sustained shared thinking referred to earlier in this chapter will support these processes. Nor can the role of a rich and varied experience be overstated. Everyone working with young children is responsible for laying the foundations of all future learning – that means we must help children to embrace novelty, excitement and challenge. (This inevitably applies to all – whatever their sensory or physical impairment. Access to experiences must be safeguarded for every child.)

Practitioners can support children's problem-finding and problem-solving by:

▶ Observing children's problem-finding and problem-solving in order to identify the strategies they are using and the progress they are making. Are they, for example:

  ▶ Making choices and decisions rather than selecting resources randomly?
  ▶ Able to explain or justify decisions?
  ▶ Being increasingly systematic – selecting what they need before embarking on an investigation or putting things away thoughtfully?
  ▶ Making a plan? Do they prepare?
  ▶ Prepared to try another approach if the first doesn't work?
  ▶ Sometimes trying again even when something does work – setting a new challenge? Perhaps doing it faster, or in a different direction?
  ▶ Sometimes selecting mathematical tools – tape measures, stop watches, etc.?

▶ Making sure that the learning environment is supportive, accepting children's successes and failures.
▶ Really listening and offering comments and suggestions that are based on what children are trying to do. These might include:

  ▶ Tell me about. . . .
  ▶ I wonder what will happen next.
  ▶ I wonder what would happen if. . . .

▶ Asking questions to promote reflective thought such as:

  ▶ What will you need?
  ▶ What was the first thing you did?
  ▶ What did you notice . . . ?
  ▶ Can you guess . . . ?
  ▶ What could we try next?

(based on Gifford 2005; Skinner 2005; and BEAM 1997)

ABSTRACT THINKING

Throughout this book the importance of abstract thinking has been emphasised. As we saw in Chapter 2, the development of abstract thought relies on communication (which will be further explored in the next chapter) and imagination (which was the focus of Chapter 5). Symbolisation and visualisation have been underlying themes throughout this chapter and the previous chapter. It is clear that effective early childhood practice must offer children opportunities to develop not only practical or concrete experience, but the mental images that will help them to begin to see things 'in their minds' eye'.

A number of possible strategies for doing this, informally and in small groups, are listed below:

1   Place a number of objects in a container, adding or subtracting a number and asking children to guess how many are left in the container. You might use:

   ▶ beanbags or soft balls in a bin/box;
   ▶ beans in an egg cup;
   ▶ toys in a box or bag;
   ▶ toy animals in a box.

2   Put imaginary objects in an imaginary box to encourage children to envisage things that are not present. Some suggested ideas are:

   ▶ enough apples to balance an elephant;
   ▶ enough children to hold hands all around the school;
   ▶ enough Lego to build the town hall;
   ▶ a jug big enough to hold all the water in a swimming pool;
   ▶ a thousand Smarties;
   ▶ a cake big enough to hold 100 giant candles for a giant's hundredth birthday;
   ▶ a toy for an ant;
   ▶ enough ant footsteps to get all the way along the corridor.

3   Trying to decide what might fit inside a particular box or bag:

   ▶ entirely imaginative (I've got a box the size of. . . . What can I put in it?);

61

> ► deciding on the best fit for a particular purpose, such as which animals featured in *Dear Zoo* (Campbell 1985) will best fit inside which box;
>
> ► for practical purposes, e.g. sending a real parcel to a real person. Encourage children to guess first.

4 Put pictures in children's minds:

> ► I'm holding a big round pizza and I cut it in halves. What shape are the two pieces?
>
> ► I'm thinking of four sweets and I want to share them with my friend – how many can we each have?
>
> ► You're standing on number five on the number line and you take two steps. Which number are you on?

5 Describe objects that can't be seen, for example:

> ► placing one of a pair of objects in a sock or bag, asking a child to describe it and asking children to find its 'twin';
>
> ► describing an unseen object in a feely bag;
>
> ► letting children guess what might be in a box according to the sound it makes or the kind of box it is, what it's made of . . .

6 Gradually unfold pieces of cloth, asking children to:

> ► tell you what it reminds them of, e.g. ice cream, sandwich, house . . .; and/or
>
> ► predict what shape it will be when completely unfolded.

7 Show children cardboard boxes that have been folded flat (nets) and ask them to guess what the three-dimensional shape will look like, or present children with nets and 3D boxes and ask them to match them up.

METACOGNITION

Some American writers (including Gardner 2006) refer to this as *metathinking*. It simply means being able to think about thinking. Edward de Bono has been particularly influential and his notion of 'six thinking hats' (for more information see www.edwdebono.com) has highlighted the value of learning to think in different ways in order to take different perspectives. Children can be helped to do this as demonstrated by the work of organisations such as Capture Arts (for more information see www.capturearts.org), which has achieved good results in the creative arts working with young children in early years settings.

In relation to mathematical thinking, the Primary National Strategy for numeracy has consistently promoted the idea of encouraging children in Key Stages 1 and 2 to explain how they arrive at the answer to a question or problem. The process is not always easy for children who initially are inclined to answer the question 'How do you know?' with a shrug and a response of 'I don't know.' However, what helps children to engage with this process is:

> Asking 'How do you know?' whether children give the right or the wrong answer. Learning to think about how their thinking worked is perhaps even more valuable for children when they have the right answer.

> Giving support and encouragement in achieving an answer that others can understand. This helps to clarify the child's own thinking for themselves as well as others. This, in turn, can help children to draw on their experience, recalling at some future point the strategies they have previously used.

> Being supportive when wrong answers are offered. Children need to feel safe enough to take risks; secure enough to be confident among adults and children and creative enough to try out new ideas.

> Encouraging guessing. Unless a child has a 'have-a-go' attitude there is nothing adults can discuss or work on, so the initial guess, hypothesis, estimate or whatever you like to call it, opens up the discussion and opens a window on thinking for children and adults.

All of these points apply to children of almost any age who are in even the very early stages of problem-solving, reasoning and numeracy. Guess first and then check – you'll be surprised how often you come close to the answer. Mathematical thinking requires a mixture of approaches – making mathematical connections, recognising relationships between everyday experiences and mathematical concepts, using a wide range of skills including sorting, matching and logic. It relies on mathematical experiences that promote the identification of patterns; problem-finding and problem-solving and the development of abstract thought through both concrete and imaginary experiences. It also relies on social and emotional contexts that encourage confident guessing and risk-taking.

63

KEY POINTS

There are many kinds of thinking, but the roots of all thought are physical, cultural and emotional. Practitioners need to support children in developing a range of strategies for problem-finding and problem-solving, to promote the development of abstract thought and to encourage thinking about thinking.

Chapter 7

Talking maths

Too often children's own insights into complex concepts are seen as trivial, stupid, or simply wrong . . . [but] children are capable of exploring complicated concepts in subtle and profound ways.

(Hall and Martello 1996: vi)

In this chapter you will:

▶ examine the importance of language in the development of thinking and learning mathematically;

▶ consider some practical guidance on promoting sustained mathematical conversations with children and on ways of promoting mathematical language in play and activities across the curriculum.

Although this chapter focuses on talk, it is crucial to bear in mind that it is *communication* that develops thought (Goldschmied and Selleck 1996). Although communication generally implies talk, many other factors are involved. Communication with others may involve signs (formal or informal); gesture; facial expression; body language; as well as speech. As we have seen, these elements of communication contribute to the development of thinking – including mathematical thinking.

This underlines the fact that although spoken language is of great importance, it is not the only means of communicating with others. EYFS draws attention to the need to overcome barriers to learning. Early years practitioners need to be aware of the benefits of signed language (such as BSL and Makaton) and graphic symbol systems (such as BLISS and REBUS) for children who have sensory impairments or expressive language difficulties.

65

There is growing awareness that communicating – by whatever means – with others brings us in touch with other minds (Siegel 1999; Hobson 2002). As babies and toddlers become more aware of the views or thoughts of others, their understanding of the world grows. They learn from studying the full range of communicative strategies (including facial expressions, gestures and body language) used by those who are important to them what to think about the world about them. Even those children who are developing spoken language in the normal way pay detailed attention not simply to the words that adults use but to all the non-verbal cues that support their growing understanding of their world (Donaldson 1986).

This has important implications for adults supporting children's developing mathematical thinking and learning. Since so many early years practitioners, in common with many members of the general public, lack confidence in mathematics this can all too easily be communicated, even unwittingly, to children. So it is important that, in talking about mathematics with young children, adults are enthusiastic – and that this is reflected in their facial expressions, their choice of words and their body language.

DEVELOPING MATHEMATICAL LANGUAGE

Mathematics uses language in a specialised way. Even words that seem ordinary and everyday to adults can seem confusing to children. As discussed in Chapter 2, the counting words themselves are used in a variety of ways and contexts. In addition, terms such as 'take-away', 'altogether' or 'sharing' may have very different mathematical meanings than the ones with which children are familiar. Communication in all its forms is essential in helping children to sort out possible confusions and develop the concepts that underpin mathematical thinking and learning. Talk, open-ended conversation and discussion are vital elements in this process.

In this section, ways of supporting young children's development of mathematical language will be explored. The focus will be on three main aspects:

1   something mathematical to talk about;
2   someone to talk to about mathematics; and
3   supportive adults.

Something mathematical to talk about

Having something to talk about depends on being engaged in things that are interesting, stimulating and exciting. This does not mean that children need always to be talking – opportunities for quiet reflection often provide the something to talk about. It does, however, underline the point made earlier (in Chapter 3) that there should be challenges and surprises in the learning environment and the learning opportunities it offers.

In the foundation stage, practitioners should be offering experiences that broaden children's horizons, laying foundations for all future learning. Children will be stimulated by experiences that are real for them and that engage them and which give them the opportunity to talk about things that matter to them. Sam, building a huge and elaborate block structure, is approached by an adult who has been told that there is not enough maths going on. She therefore wants to get Sam talking about maths and immediately begins asking questions about what shape the blocks are, how many blocks Sam has used and whether his structure is taller or shorter than various objects around the room.

Sam does not respond. Why not? Block building has many inherently mathematical qualities to do with size, shape, space, measures, number, ratio, pattern and so on – but Sam's focus is not on these elements at this time. While he is building he is engaged with the story he is telling himself. This involves a great deal of mathematical language – positional language, comparative language, number and calculation, but it also involves imagination and at this stage in the process it is this that motivates Sam. Later, when he has an opportunity to reflect on his experience and learning, it may be easier to promote mathematical vocabulary and discussion.

Despite the fact that several reports (see for example Sammons *et al.* 2002) have suggested that there is insufficient mathematics going on in the foundation stage, since 'maths is about life' it is an area of learning that is difficult to avoid. What often happens, as was perhaps the case with the adult supporting Sam, is that adults forget that maths talk does not only involve number, calculation, shape, space and measures. It includes problem-solving, reasoning, identifying patterns, predictions, categorisation, as well as all the elements (especially imagination) that contribute to abstract thinking.

The continuous provision offered by an early years setting – the things that are always available such as sand, water, blocks, role play and wheeled toys – help children to feel secure by providing a secure predictable

67

framework. However, if that context becomes too predictable it can be seen as boring. Adults need to ensure (as discussed in Chapter 5) that resources are supplemented with things that encourage children to look with new eyes, to see things afresh, to begin a different cycle of exploration. This can be achieved by adding something as simple as some new pictures of unusual vehicles or exotic buildings to the block area. It could be a tray of unusual shells together with some photographs, postcards and books that will encourage discussion of pattern, or it might be that teddy can't get all his belongings into the suitcase for his holiday.

Such stimulation might come from a link with home. This could be photographs of mathematical aspects of the neighbourhood. One setting had a large collection of such photos and had printed them with increasing focus on one small element. There was, for example, a picture of a whole street, a single house in that street, the door on that house and the number on the door. Another set focused on shape – a bus in a street, a bus in close-up, rectangular windows.

Some resources might also focus on things children have at home. Photographs of family members are common – but the construction area might also include photos of children playing with different construction toys at home. Discussion can then focus on similarities and differences. But, of course, as discussed in Chapter 3, many of the things that children are excited and stimulated by are special to them. Provision should take account of these preferences or idiosyncrasies. Because maths is about life, practitioners can allow children to work and play with whatever they are most interested in and develop the curriculum from that starting point. In Chapter 6 the wide range of mathematical learning opportunities that exist in an early years setting was highlighted. All that is required is to ensure that they are all so exciting, so real to children and so well-resourced as to ensure that they want to communicate their mathematical ideas.

Someone to talk to about mathematics

Even in a rich mathematical environment, children need to feel confident about talking to others. Some of this confidence comes from being in a supportive atmosphere where children feel known and valued, and where it is all right to make mistakes and learn from them. But often it comes down to ensuring that children are given real opportunities to talk.

In order to ensure that children have someone to talk to, adults need to enable children to work and play in small groups. Although large groups may have a place in the foundation stage in developing a sense of community, they are unhelpful in developing language. Language is a developmental process and as such needs to be practised. Children of three years of age in a group of twenty or more have very little opportunity to use talk. They may, if they don't simply 'switch off', hear some language in a story or song, but they will not have an opportunity to communicate. Communication must be a two-way process involving both talking and listening.

The younger the child the more important it is to ensure that the groups in which they come together are small. It has been suggested that the optimum size for groups to promote interaction and communication is twice the child's age. So for two-year-olds, genuine communication is most likely to occur in a group of four and for five-year-olds in a group of ten. Most group activities in most early years settings are significantly larger than this. This often happens for organisational reasons – perhaps to allow staff to take a break or prepare for lunch. If this cannot be overcome in any other way, then practitioners should ensure that such times are kept to a minimum, otherwise children will find it difficult to find anyone to talk to about mathematics or anything else.

The organisation of the room also has an impact on the way in which children group themselves – and thus the extent to which they feel able to talk. Children – like adults – often feel more comfortable about talking when they have a small space in which to talk. You have only to picture yourself walking into a doctor's waiting room to know how uncomfortable it can feel to talk within a large group of people you don't know well. Rooms that have small tables with just a couple of chairs; quiet spaces with some interesting resources set out enticingly; or areas and materials from which children can create dens are likely to promote conversation. When materials and experiences that promote mathematical thinking and learning are readily available, much of the conversation is likely to be about mathematics.

There are, of course, some children who find it difficult to make social contact with others in any grouping and they will need help to develop strategies for getting into other children's games and conversations. Another role for adults is undoubtedly to offer models for talking about maths. They can provide new vocabulary, pose challenging questions and draw children's attention to particular aspects of mathematics, such as a pattern that seems to be emerging in children's music-making. However, adults should not fall into the trap of thinking that the development of mathematical language rests entirely with them. Young children's

69

conversation with other children offers them opportunities to try things out, get things wrong and to learn from others. Adults can gain much insight into children's understanding of key mathematical vocabulary and their mathematical understanding by observing and listening to the interactions that occur between children when adults are not intervening.

Vivian Gussin Paley (1981: 13) records a conversation between Wally (W) and Eddie (E) about measurement as they plan to play 'Jack and the Beanstalk':

W: The big rug is the giant's castle. The small one is Jack's house.

E: Both rugs are the same.

W: They can't be the same. Watch me. I'll walk around the rug. Now watch – walk, walk, walk, walk, walk, walk, walk, walk, walk – count all those walks. Okay. Now count the other rug. Walk, walk, walk, walk, walk. See? That one has more walks.

E: No fair. You cheated. You walked faster.

W: I don't have to walk. I can just look.

E: I can look too. But you have to measure it. You need a ruler. About six hundred inches or feet.

W: We have a ruler.

E: Not that one. Not the short kind. You have to use the long kind that gets curled up in a box.

W: Use people. People's bodies. Lying down in a row.

E: That's a great idea. I never even thought of that.

This conversation demonstrates both a wide range of knowledge and some misconceptions. It is highly unlikely that such a conversation could have taken place in a large group – even if it did, try to imagine what the other ten or twenty children would be doing. It is also unlikely that such a conversation would occur with an adult present. All but the most skilled (and the most confident) adults would feel that they needed to interject, to correct misconceptions and to offer alternatives. In fact Vivian Gussin Paley does go on to offer some advice but over several days, children fail to trust the answer supplied by the tape measure she provides, commenting that 'rulers aren't really real, are they?'

Above all, adults have to remember that children's conversations with other children (and with themselves) offer a perspective that conversation with an adult does not. By rehearsing these misconceptions children come to a better understanding. They are able to challenge their own and other children's misconceptions. In the dialogue between Eddie and Wally, Eddie is able to say 'not that one' – a phrase which if it came from an adult could demolish a child's confidence. Coming from another child it has a different impact.

Supportive adults

Adults need to support the process of developing language in both direct and indirect ways. Indirectly, as we have already seen, they need to support maths talk by:

▶ planning a learning environment that supports mathematical activity with rich resources, indoors and out and in a wide range of areas of provision;

▶ supporting children who may have difficulty in making social contact with others;

▶ ensuring that there are small spaces that promote children's interaction and conversation.

In addition, adults need to plan their own time to ensure that they are able to observe children's mathematical learning as well as intervening in situations where they can support or enhance the development of mathematical thinking and learning.

Interventions that promote genuine communication and conversation are not easy to achieve and require sensitive, experienced and reflective practitioners. Effective and communicative interventions can take a number of forms. Listening to children is probably the best starting point, but sometimes you might need to have some strategies for getting children talking. The ways in which adults talk to children can affect the way in which children respond. Questioning is perhaps the most common strategy that adults in early childhood settings use as an intervention strategy, but it is not always effective. Clearly, in the sections that follow there is some overlap, but the points raised are intended to get you thinking about how you intervene and how effective your interventions are in helping children to think and learn about mathematics.

GETTING CHILDREN TALKING

Livingstone (2005) offers four tips (aimed primarily at parents) for getting children to talk:

▶ Be chatty. The children of chatty parents can have up to 300 extra words at the age of two.

▶ Talk about the things your child is paying attention to.

▶ Don't ask unnecessary questions. More often than not, if your child knows the answer she doesn't need to be asked the question, and if she doesn't there's no point in asking.

▶ Listen to your child and use your talking to extend what she says rather than starting a new topic.

These are helpful for any adult working with young children but the four points do need to be seen as a group rather than taken in isolation. Simply being chatty won't help – but if you focus on what the child is already doing and show that you're interested, children are more likely to join in. You will see as you work through these sections that there are what appear to be contradictions. You will shortly be given advice to remain silent (based on Durkin 2001) – but that needs to be seen alongside periods of general chattiness. In fact these four points offer good principles as a starting point for enhanced mathematical conversations. Similarly, although you shouldn't ask unnecessary questions, some questions are particularly helpful in setting off a conversation. Language is just like that – there isn't a recipe or one single answer. In order to engage reluctant talkers, adults have to try a number of strategies. It is important for children to be comfortable in talking since it gives us (and them) a window on their thinking. It is also important to develop mathematical talk in particular, since it allows for the development of mathematical vocabulary – ways of talking about maths. It also allows adults to support children in developing mathematical ways of thinking and learning – problem-solving, reasoning, hypothesising and so on.

LISTENING

Much has been written about children learning to listen. In fact, perhaps the most important part of learning to listen comes from being listened to. Busy adults can be very bad at really listening to what children are saying. Often we pretend to listen or only give children limited attention rather than our full attention (Miles 1994). As a practitioner, if this is happening regularly the staff team should review practice in order to ensure that adults can engage more fully with children, since true listening is a vital part of communication, thinking and learning. Effective listening might include the following strategies:

▶ Assume that when children are trying to tell you something they have something sensible to say.

▶ Ask for an explanation if you don't understand, or sometimes better still try to put into your own words what you think they are trying to say and checking whether you've got it right. This is sometimes called 'reflective listening' (Livingstone 2005).

▶ Take time – don't try to rush the child or rush your responses. Don't be afraid of some silences, they can give a child vital thinking time.

EFFECTIVE TALKING

Communication is a two-way process and requires adults and children to talk and to listen. Developing the sustained, shared thinking that comes from genuine conversations relies on a number of things, which were discussed in Chapter 6. Developing children's ability to enjoy and engage in communication with others depends at least in part on adults' ability to:

▶ Encourage play and playfulness. Young children enjoy humour, and humorous exchanges often support extended conversation. Encouraging them to think of a wide range of possible (and impossible) answers can support imagination, which in turn contributes to abstract thought and to creative problem-solving.

▶ Allow sufficient time and tolerate some silence – recognising that some important thinking might be going on.

▶ Resist lecturing or giving orders. Instead offer some choices or encourage children to think about solutions. At a stage in their lives when young children are trying to become independent, shouting or ordering are rarely the best way to go about developing a conversation.

▶ Resist opening a conversation with a question. When adults ask questions children tend to believe that they have some reason for asking them – so if a child knows the answer to your question he or she might simply be suspicious about why you're asking. It's usually better to begin with a statement such as 'What a long road you've built . . .' or 'I can't believe how long you've been working on this model . . .'.

▶ Give children a range of opportunities to develop the use of mathematical language by:

- allowing them to hear and practise mathematical language in a range of contexts, including reading and telling stories with a mathematical focus (see, for example, Bromley 2005; Featherstone 2005);
- becoming sufficiently confident to try out mathematical vocabulary;
- describing, defining and comparing mathematical properties – talking about positions, methods, patterns, relationships, rules;
- discussing ways that they have gone about solving (or finding) problems;
- promoting predicting, estimating, guessing;
- encouraging them to explain or justify ideas, reasons, approaches;
- having the opportunity to respond to questions that promote different kinds of thinking.

▶ Encourage constant questioning. At home, children do most of the questioning and it is a vital strategy in their quest to know more and understand their world better. In group settings adults tend to take on the role of questioner. Although it is helpful to model different ways of asking questions, curiosity and questioning can also be stimulated through interesting books, objects, materials and pictures. We can also encourage children's questions by:

- analysing their questions (e.g. What do you mean by . . .?);
- rephrasing the question to check for shared understanding;
- turning the question back to the child;
- asking a supporting question (e.g. I wonder whether . . .);
- suggesting a line of enquiry (e.g. Perhaps we could . . .).

QUESTIONING

In general it is said that open-ended questions are more helpful than closed questions in supporting the development of mathematical thinking and learning. Although this is generally true, on some occasions a closed question can 'break the ice' and get children talking. This depends, of course, on knowing the children you work with and identifying the best strategies for promoting mathematical talk. But don't forget that sometimes personal statements produce more response in children than questions! Your statements allow *children* to ask questions. Below is a list of questions that might extend mathematical language and thought:

▶ How could we . . .?
▶ Can you tell me a different way . . .?
▶ What does this make you think of?
▶ What could you try next?
▶ How are you going to . . .?
▶ What do you think it might be?
▶ How did you find that out?
▶ Why do you think that . . .?
▶ How would you describe it?
▶ What's the difference between . . .?
▶ How are they the same?
▶ How are they different?
▶ Do you mean . . .?
▶ Why did you choose . . .?

KEY POINTS

The development of mathematical language shapes and influences mathematical thinking. Children need to have something to talk about and someone to talk to in order to develop mathematical thinking and learning. Adults need to use strategies that get children talking, including listening and questioning.

Chapter 8

Creative maths

Using storytelling was very gripping, the children were totally engrossed. . . . The children are more inspired and therefore more interested in what they are doing. As it is so practical they are all remembering more and I feel they are beginning to make more links in their learning.

(Teachers' comments included
in Lee and Pound 2005)

In this chapter you will:

▶ focus on the importance of creative arts to the development of mathematical thinking;
▶ consider the role of imaginative or dramatic play, story, song and rhyme, music and dance, and the visual arts in developing mathematical understanding;
▶ explore the role of symbolic representation in mathematical thinking and learning.

The focus of this chapter will be the creative arts – the aspects highlighted in the area of learning and development known as creative development (DfES 2007). This does not mean that creativity is limited to the use of creative media or that only the arts are creative. Mathematics (and the sciences) involves a great deal of creative thinking. However, the creative arts do have a particular role to play in helping children and adults to symbolise their ideas. Like playing and talking, creative media offer another way of learning to think mathematically.

Current understandings about the role that aspects of creative learning and development can play in supporting mathematical thinking and learning have evolved from a number of sources. Some of these are research based, others are based on philosophical principles. Since this is an aspect of mathematics that is gaining growing recognition, a rationale or explanation of the thinking on which it is based is shown below. This should serve as background information to the rest of the chapter. References for each aspect or area of research are given in Table 7.1 to enable you to follow up or challenge the ideas should you wish to do so.

In summary, adopting creative approaches to mathematical thinking and learning can therefore be justified in a number of ways:

▶ The development of narrative in story and play helps children to make sense of the world, including the mathematical world.

▶ Thinking and learning are not simply the domain of the brain or head. They may depend on a range of intelligences, on physical action and emotional engagement (or motivation). Using music, dance, painting, drawing and modelling allows children to think in a variety of ways (a topic that was explored in Chapter 6).

▶ In addition to spoken language, imaginative play, music and dance, stories and visual representations enable children to symbolise their understandings in a variety of ways (as suggested by the hundred languages of children (Malaguzzi 1995)).

CREATIVE APPROACHES TO MATHEMATICS

The directors of MakeBelieve Arts, a theatre-in-education company in south London, were heavily influenced by Egan's (1988) view that anything, even mathematics, could be taught through story. They developed an approach initially aimed at children in Key Stage 1, which they entitled *Dramatic Mathematics*. Taking Egan's work as their starting point they developed stories and a teachers' resource pack (Lee and Tompsett 2004). Small groups of actors presented five different interactive stories to classes of children that together addressed virtually the whole of the mathematics curriculum for Key Stage 1. This was highly successful, but it was felt that although children gained immensely from the sessions, story and drama would be more effectively integrated into the curriculum if teachers felt more able to develop their own creative approaches to mathematics.

INSET sessions were developed to support teachers in the foundation stage and at Key Stage 1 in developing stories and in creating other opportunities to integrate creative arts into the maths curriculum. There was an emphasis on adults creating their own stories, sometimes in

TABLE 8.1 Theoretical rationale for adopting creative approaches to mathematics

Area of research and thinking underlining the value of creative approaches to mathematical thinking and learning	Relevant references	Comments
The importance of narrative in supporting learning	Egan 1988; Paley 1990	Psycholinguistic research demonstrated the importance of narrative in human learning. Kieran Egan (1988) claimed that anything, even mathematics, could be taught through story to any age group. He offered a model to enable teachers to create their own stories. Vivian Gussin Paley (1990), on the other hand, demonstrated that children's own stories could be used as the basis of the curriculum.
Importance of narrative in teaching and learning mathematics	Devlin 2000; Schiro 2004; Whitin and Wilde 1995	Mathematicians (Devlin 2000) and educationalists have taken up these ideas. Whitin and Wilde (1995) focus on the use of books and story in promoting mathematical understanding in the primary years (including the equivalent of the foundation stage). Schiro (2004) makes similar claims for his work with older students in the equivalent of middle and secondary schools.
Importance of a range of inter-dependent multiple intelligences	Gardner 1999	Howard Gardner's work on multiple intelligences has been highly acclaimed since its initial publication early in the 1980s. His theory that humans have a number of different intelligences, including what he terms logical-mathematical intelligence, has been influential in leading educationalists to consider the different ways in which humans learn – making use of different intelligences, including linguistic and bodily-kinaesthetic intelligences.
Increased understanding of the role of physicality in learning	Gardner 1999; Bresler 2004; Eliot 1999	Since the publication of his first book (Gardner 1983) on the subject, neuroscientific research has increasingly underlined the importance of physical (or bodily-kinaesthetic) aspects of learning. Some studies (Eliot 1999) highlighted the importance of physical action in infancy, but others (see, for example, Bresler 2004) have claimed a role for physicality in learning throughout life.

Increased understanding of the role of emotions in learning	Gardner 1983; Goleman 1996; Eliot 1999; Gerhardt 2004	Again it was Gardner who drew attention to the importance of the emotional and social aspects of learning and development (interpersonal and intrapersonal intelligences). Daniel Goleman (1996) took this up and it is his term 'emotional intelligence' that has been so influential in many aspects of public consciousness over the past ten years. Neuroscientific evidence increasingly supports the close relationship between social and emotional well-being and learning (Gopnik *et al.* 1999). Story (as discussed in Chapter 5) allows children to explore emotion and knowledge simultaneously. Whitin and Wilde (1995: 106) include in their book, teachers' comments on using story to support mathematical learning. One teacher comments that 'mathematical thinkers are interested in the thinking of others', while another says 'giving children the opportunity to wonder about things and to further investigate their "wonders" makes them more excited about learning and thus gives them a much more active involvement in their own learning'.
Learning supported by symbolic representation or 'tools for thinking'	Egan 1989; Gardner 1993; Malaguzzi 1995; Rogoff 2003	Egan (1989) suggests that the most effective tools for thinking (or forms of symbolic representation) when working with young children are story, song and rhyme. Rogoff (2003: 262) describes the way in which different cultures favour different tools for thinking. She goes on to explain how the tools for thinking that are selected shape the thinking itself. She gives an example from mathematics. She writes that: 'when mathematics is used for practical purposes – such as by vendors, carpenters, farmers and dieters – people seldom come up with nonsense results in their calculations. However, calculations in the context of schooling regularly produce some absurd errors, with results that are impossible if the meaning of the problem being solved is considered'. The use of symbolic representations with which early childhood practitioners are probably most familiar occurs in Reggio Emilia, in Northern Italy. The approach to early education adopted there refers to 'the 100 languages of children' (Malaguzzi 1995). The curriculum is based on using a wide variety of forms of symbolic representation (music, dance, 2D and 3D art, talk, etc.) to support all learning and development – including mathematical understanding.
The role of imagination in supporting abstract thought	Jenkinson 2001; Ramachandran 2003; Devlin 2000; Mazur 2003	Jenkinson (2001) reminds us that since imagination is innate, a feature of childhood everywhere, it must have a biological function. Ramachandran (2003) points to the importance of metaphor to imagination and creative thinking as important aspects of human learning. Mathematicians (Devlin 2000; Mazur 2003) have also developed a keen interest in imagination as part of the process of thinking in the abstract.

collaboration with children, using and adapting known books and stories, on promoting role play and problem-solving, and on developing and modifying music, songs and rhymes or poetry to reinforce the mathematical thinking and learning.

Subsequent work was cross-phase involving children from foundation stage to year 4. It focused in particular on giants – a rich source of mathematical investigation and curiosity. The fact that there was so much interest, not only from adults working in the foundation stage, but also with significantly older children, is an indication of changing views of learning and teaching. Physical action, the use of imagination and symbolic representation, and the recognition that all learning involves emotional engagement (both negative and positive) are being more widely recognised as vital for all areas of learning and development, even (or perhaps especially) mathematics.

In the sections that follow, there are some ideas about how you can develop more creative approaches to mathematics with the children whose mathematical thinking and learning you are supporting.

Story, dramatic play and mathematics

Traditional stories are widely used to support mathematical thinking and learning. Role play areas that allow children to explore the story of 'Goldilocks and the Three Bears' are a rich seam for learning about number, shape, space and measures within foundation stage provision. The story of the 'Three Billy-goats Gruff' is more commonly acted out either in group times or as part of small-world play provision.

There are any number of books on the market that can be used to support mathematical thinking and learning. Table 7.2 sets out a few ideas for using narrative to support mathematical thinking and learning, but you might also like to refer to Helen Bromley's (2005) or Sally Featherstone's (2005) books for further ideas.

The wealth of children's books available should not mean that practitioners ignore children's own stories. Vivian Gussin Paley (1990) has probably done more than any other writer to highlight the importance of the stories children create, basing her curriculum on the children's stories told to and scribed by her. Children's stories are then acted out by other children – a process that can give rise to mathematical discussion and enhance mathematical understanding. In her work the focus is very much on children's social and emotional development, but the following

TABLE 8.2 Picture books that can be used as starting points to develop mathematical thinking and learning

Aspect of problem-solving, reasoning and numeracy	Book title, author and date of publication	Comment	Dramatic play opportunity to support mathematical learning
Numbers	*Hippos Go Berserk* (Boynton 2000)	A counting book ostensibly counting from one to nine and back again. But it has a storyline – which means that children get involved in calculation too.	Magnetic board with large number of laminated paper hippos, plus paper hats and balloons for the party – all with magnetic strip attached. (This could also be done with Velcro dots and a fabric board.)
Calculation	*One is a Snail, Ten is a Crab* (Sayre and Sayre 2004)	Again a counting book, but one that makes calculation irresistible. Although it does not have an overt storyline, the illustrations depict beach scenes that suggest a context to the reader.	Small-world provision – snail shells, people, dogs, insects, spiders and crabs – together with some towels, shells, seaweed.
Shape, space and measures	*Where's my Teddy?* (Alborough 2004)	Great opportunities for discussion of comparative size.	Collection of dolls of different sizes (including small-world people) and teddies of different sizes.
Problem-solving/ problem-finding	*The Secret Path* (Butterworth 2003)	The theme of this book is a maze, and there is a large fold-out page depicting the maze and inviting children to find a way through.	A laminated copy of the maze with small-world figures depicted in the story (fox, rabbit, etc.) and wipe-clean pens of different colours to trace the routes.
Guessing or predicting	*The Great Pet Sale* (Inkpen 2006)	Amusing story that provides opportunities for discussing money as well as flaps that invite predictions.	Pet shop role play with price tickets.
Developing abstract thinking	*Come Away from the Water Shirley* (Burningham 1992)	Pictures show both what is happening on the beach and what is going on in Shirley's imagination.	Figures in the water tray could be used to explore mathematical potential of this dual story, challenging children's thinking and making them more aware of thinking about thinking.
Identifying and creating pattern	*Harry and the Robots* (Whybrow and Reynolds 2003)	The beginning and end papers of this book have a series of robots set out in patterns.	Making a collection of robots using different patterns and setting them out in different patterns.

story (collected as part of the work of MakeBelieve Arts) can be used to highlight a child's interest in time and sequence:

> Once there was a little girl. The little girl plant a flower and the flower didn't grow. So she make another flower and she put in two seeds and then she water it and then she waited. And it didn't grow. And she wait and it didn't grow. So she wait and wait for a long time. And when its night she still waiting. And it didn't grow. And the seed and the water died. And her mum sent her to bed.
>
> (MakeBelieve Arts 2007: 8)

Similarly, another child's story about a dragon includes the words 'he sleeps for a long whole week up to one hundred days' (MakeBelieve Arts 2007: 20). This not only offers an opportunity for the child to explore the language and concept of time, it also gives the adults supporting him or her a way of understanding what the child understands and thus finding ways to support further development.

One important way to promote children's own stories and their general interest in narrative is for the adults themselves to create their own stories. Egan's approach (1988) is to identify what he terms 'binary opposites' around which to focus the story, and many of these (such as sadness–happiness; hopes–fears) are of an affective or emotional nature. This, of course, underlines the way in which all learning is connected to emotions – even mathematics. A simpler model for creating stories has been termed 'hand plot development' (Lee and Pound 2005: 15). The five fingers of one hand are used to remind the storyteller that a good story has five parts – introduction, development, conflict, climax and conclusion. (It is further suggested that a very good story also involves truth, lies and exaggeration.) In the familiar story of 'Goldilocks and the Three Bears' the five key elements might be:

Introduction	The bears go out
Development	Goldilocks arrives
Conflict	Things get broken
Climax	The bears come home
Conclusion	Goldilocks runs away.

(I leave it to you to decide what the truth, lies and exaggerations are.)

Stories – whether published, told by children or created by adults – can be developed in a number of ways. The telling and retelling of stories may involve dramatic play (both formal and informal; large-scale role play or involving small-world figures), music and dance, paintings and drawings, models and sculptures. The process of translating ideas from one creative medium to another supports children's thinking.

Music and mathematics

The notion that music supports memory has already been cited as one reason why the two areas of learning of music and mathematics should be linked. The use of music to support mathematical learning need not stop at counting songs. As discussed in Chapter 5, songs can be adapted and modified to cover the whole curriculum for problem-solving, reasoning and numeracy. Songs, like stories, can also support the development of mathematical vocabulary by providing children with a bank of ready-made phrases and ideas on which they can draw in play and in conversation.

The use of musical instruments presents another mathematical opportunity. Large and small instruments; or instruments with similar shapes that create sounds in different ways (blowing, plucking, banging, shaking and so on) offer excellent opportunities for both musical and mathematical discussion. Pitched instruments such as xylophones and glockenspiels demonstrate the way in which size is related to pitch – the smaller the note the higher it sounds. Versions of these instruments can be purchased that place the high notes higher than the low notes (such as step chime bars). The same relationship can be demonstrated using plastic drain pipe cut to different lengths. Boomwhackers can also be purchased – exciting lengths of coloured plastic cut to different sizes and therefore playing different notes.

Music and mathematics share some vocabulary, such as 'long' and 'short', and it can be stimulating to discuss this with children. Interestingly 'high' and 'low' have apparently different meanings – a high note in music is small whereas a high number is a large one. Don't be afraid to explore these anomalies – some children will be very stimulated by such discussion. One important aspect of the relationship between music and mathematics is that both operate in time *and* space. So, activities that explore concepts such as long and short, fast and slow, loud or quiet can contribute to both areas of learning.

There are two further vital reasons for linking music and mathematics, and it is difficult to know which is more important. First, they are commonly linked because they have pattern in common (Gardner 1999).

As pointed out in Chapter 4, if mathematics is the science of pattern, music and dance are the arts of pattern. Symmetry, structure, repeating elements, cyclical elements, aspects that ascend and descend are common to both disciplines and this means that learning in one area can support learning in the other.

Second, music and maths should be linked because singing, dancing and music-making can make mathematics more playful. Although we claim that children learn through play, mathematics learning and teaching is rarely playful. Playing music can help mathematics to become much more enjoyable and fun for adults and children.

Visual arts and mathematics

Both two- and three-dimensional art offers opportunities to develop mathematical understanding. Using a malleable material, such as clay, allows children to experience the way in which a given quantity can change shape and size, or can be changed and then made to revert to its original shape. Printing gives children the opportunity to focus on perimeter and area – marking the boundaries and filling the whole of the paper. Creative media enable children to explore pattern.

It has long been accepted that the marks which children make – whether with paints or pencils, charcoal or chalk, gravy or ice cream – carry meaning (see, for example, Matthews 2003). As in play, children's informal mark-making gives adults a window on the thinking and under-standing of the children with whom they are working. Young children's mark-making has been extensively studied and valued in relation to the development of literacy but has not been widely seen as having the same importance for the development of mathematical understanding. Worthington and Carruthers (2003) have undertaken research looking at the role of children's mark-making in both shaping and identifying children's mathematical thinking and understanding.

They compare children's efforts to make sense of the two worlds of mathematics – at home and in school (or other early years setting) – to bilingualism, offering the term 'bi-numeracy':

> Young children feel comfortable with their first language – the informal spoken and written marks of home. If they can gradually make sense of abstract symbols and written methods in their own way, surely they would be developing fluency in both? They'd be able to move between the two languages with understanding – like being bi-lingual.
>
> (Worthington and Carruthers 2003: 74)

Children have in fact, they suggest, to learn to translate between mathematical language and everyday language. Like the practitioners in Reggio Emilia, Worthington and Carruthers (2003) underline the importance to children's thinking and understanding of translating from one language (or creative medium) to another. Representing (or re-presenting) ideas verbally, graphically, in imaginative play or block-building enables children to think and re-think their ideas.

KEY POINTS

A range of research has highlighted the way in which creative media can support mathematical development. In this chapter, the role of narrative – printed stories, children's own stories and the stories that adults make up – can be used to enhance mathematical understanding. Mark-making, dramatic play, music and dance can all be used to support mathematical thinking and learning.

Chapter 9

Creating an environment for mathematical development

> It is essential to remember that maths happens throughout the learning environment, not only in the maths area or during activities which focus on maths. During the foundation stage, children should have opportunities to investigate number, shape, space and measures through meaningful, practical experiences, both indoors and outdoors.
>
> (Cartwright *et al.* 2002: 17)

In this chapter you will:

▶ consider provision for supporting mathematical thinking and learning indoors and out;

▶ reflect on the opportunities for developing mathematical understanding across the curriculum.

All too often, mathematics provision is limited to the maths area – which is frequently little more than an uninviting table, chairs and set of shelves or trays with pegs and peg boards, number puzzles, some plastic shapes and a number line or set of number pictures. Similarly, planning for mathematical thinking and learning is often little more than a box on the planning sheet which states that in the maths area beads and bead pattern cards will be put out. On the whole, both adults and children find this uninspiring. The most exciting mathematical event of the day can be nothing more than singing counting songs on the carpet at the end of the session.

Children deserve, and adults benefit from, a much richer and more stimulating environment in which to develop PSRN. Adults benefit because they learn more about what children can do and can become enthusiastic and innovative rather than simply acting in a routine way.

EYFS (DfES 2007: 62) suggests that mathematical understanding should be developed through:

▶ 'all children's early experiences';
▶ activities that are both intrinsically mathematical and others, such as block play, in which 'mathematical learning (can) be drawn out'; and
▶ drawing attention to the mathematics inherent in 'play and daily routines'.

Under 'Enabling Environments' for this area of learning and development, the guidance states that it is important to:

▶ Recognise the mathematical potential of the outdoor environment . . .
▶ Exploit the mathematical potential of the indoor environment . . .
▶ Ensure that mathematical resources are readily available both indoors and outside.

(DfES 2007: 61)

A mathematically rich environment needs to be resourced so that mathematics cannot be missed; so that connections are made between PSRN and the whole of life – including home, the early years setting and the wider world. In the sections that follow, suggestions for provision have been separated into those for children up to and over the age of three. These are by no means hard and fast rules. It seems important, however, to try to ensure that the introduction of EYFS does not become an excuse for top-down pressure to come to bear on our youngest children. It is a source of some regret that this area of learning and development has been renamed problem-solving, reasoning *and* numeracy. Problem-solving and reasoning are generic abilities that underpin not only maths but other areas of the curriculum, and making these the focus of this area of learning and development is to be welcomed because it highlights the links between mathematics and other aspects of life and learning.

However, a focus on numeracy for six-month-old babies, or even those of 26 months, has its dangers. It is, of course, entirely desirable for early childhood practitioners to know that babies are logical thinkers, that they are establishing 'object permanence', and that learning to classify and compare are steps towards understanding calculation. What must never be lost sight of, however, is that they are also vital steps in learning to live with others. Babies under a year of age are not only logical mathematical thinkers – they are seeking to make sense of their world – a world that is full of human contacts that are not always logical and which are often highly emotional. Although classification and comparison are essential elements of mathematical understanding and practice, they are also part of scientific thinking and understanding. Moreover, they are yet another way in which humans make sense of a complex world – making connections between sometimes disparate events and people.

In many countries of the world, young children reach the age of statutory schooling before coming across a curriculum that includes the word 'mathematics'. And yet, somehow, many of them grow up to be good mathematicians. So, as you read the sections that follow, do not lose sight of the fact that there is more to the life of a very young child than any one area of learning and development – even mathematics. In addition, young children are learning many things at once and applying learning in one area of provision to different areas of learning and development.

ROUTINES AND MATHEMATICAL THINKING AND LEARNING

Routines for children of all ages can support many aspects of mathematical thinking and learning. For babies the simple process of eating, sleeping and their personal care routines offer a cyclical pattern. But, they also offer an opportunity for adults to talk in ways that will support understanding. Repeated and familiar phrases such as:

- ▶ 'have you had enough?'
- ▶ 'just one more'
- ▶ 'all gone'.

begin to shape mathematical learning. The use of songs and rhymes at routine times also highlights pattern, rhythms and time and the vocabulary of number, shape and space. Phrases such as 'one step, two step . . . tickling under there' contain numbers and positional language.

As children get older, meal times, bath times, shopping, cooking, laundry and cleaning provide a host of opportunities for developing mathematical thinking and awareness. In group settings, registration, snack times or meal times, tidying up and sharing with others in work and play offer untold opportunities for maths. You might like to refer back to Chapter 3 (Table 3.1) where everyday and routine examples were examined for their mathematical potential.

PROVISION FOR CHILDREN UP TO THREE YEARS OF AGE

Table 9.1 identifies the areas of provision that High/Scope considers appropriate for babies and toddlers (Post and Hohmann 2000). The mathematical potential of each area for babies and toddlers is considered.

Dedicated provision both in the maths area and outdoors

EYFS (DfES 2007: 4.3) reminds us that 'children will more easily make connections between things they've learned if the environment encourages them to do so. For example, they need to be able to fetch materials easily and to be able to move them from one place to another.' Setting up a dedicated maths area can help children to know where they can find the resources they need. They should be encouraged to take the resources to wherever they need them and then replace them so that other children will also be able to find them.

An indoor maths area might include:

▶ A wide range of interesting resources for sorting, ordering, exploring and comparing, such as collections of shells, pebbles, buttons, jewels, etc. One adult had collected a vast assortment of pegs – wooden, plastic, large, small, different mechanisms, different colours and decorations. Many children became very engaged with this particular collection. These collections can also be used to explore pattern. It is important to have some large quantities of things – although children may only be able to count small numbers, they generally love big numbers – describing them as loads, heaps, mountains, zillions and so on.

▶ Maths games including materials for children to make up their own games. Hill (in Marsden and Woodbridge 2005) describes adding topic-related props (in this case penguins, polar bears, silver stars and snowflakes) to the maths area in order to stimulate not only mathematical games but a range of

89

TABLE 9.1 The mathematical potential of areas of provision for children up to the age of three

Arranging and equipping an environment for learning (based on Post and Hohmann 2000)		Supporting mathematical thinking and learning
Materials that support babies' movement	▲ moving limbs, turning over, rolling ▲ sitting ▲ scooting and crawling ▲ cruising ▲ walking, riding, rocking ▲ climbing, jumping and running	As discussed in Chapter 6, the development of mathematical thinking and learning is highly dependent on physical action. Clements (1998: 3, citing Freudenthal) writes: 'Geometry is grasping space . . . that space in which the child lives, breathes and moves. The space that the child must learn to know, explore, conquer, in order to live, breathe and move better in it'.
Resources for toddlers' movement area	▲ things to climb on and jump off ▲ things to get inside ▲ push and pull toys ▲ riding/rocking toys ▲ balls ▲ simple musical instruments/ recordings	Second, the self-confidence and the ability to take risks that physical competence gives a child (Walsh 2004) also contributes to mathematical thinking and learning. Third, rocking, spinning, swinging – all actions loved by babies and toddlers – stimulate what is known as the *vestibular system*, which 'provides a fast track into the brain' (Eliot 1999: 156), creating the heightened focus necessary to effective learning.
Materials that appeal to the senses	▲ aromatic materials and experiences ▲ sound-producing materials and experiences ▲ materials to touch, taste and look at (including natural materials; wooden objects; metal objects; objects made of leather, cloth, rubber, fur and paper/cardboard	Sensory experience is the foundation of all other learning and even newborn babies begin to make connections between different sensory stimuli (Gopnik *et al.* 1999). As suggested in Chapter 6, rich and stimulating experiences contribute to problem-solving abilities. Such materials provide the basis for later comparisons and classifications.

Sand and water area

▲ things to fill and empty
▲ things to float
▲ things to hide and find
▲ things to pretend with

These materials support mathematical thinking and learning in ways that go way beyond counting or learning about measures. They teach children about cause and effect and object permanence, and children are able to develop a range of problem-finding and problem-solving strategies and have opportunities to gather experiences that will enable them to make informed guesses. Throughout this book the importance of imaginative or pretend play to the development of abstract thinking has been stressed – the process begins in infancy.

Indoor play for babies

▲ pleasant reminders of home
▲ materials for sensory exploration and play
▲ materials that can be set in motion
▲ movement equipment
▲ books

An area such as this allows children to:

▲ feel secure and therefore open to learning (Gerhardt 2004);
▲ develop sensory awareness;
▲ learn about cause and effect and enhance spatial awareness;
▲ explore their environment and enhance their own sense of independence, agency and confidence;
▲ begin to learn all that there is to be learnt from an early love of books.

Book area

▲ board books
▲ picture books
▲ wordless books
▲ magazines, pictures, photos

As we have seen throughout this book, books and stories have immense mathematical potential. For young children the ideas of pattern, structure, sequence and representation present in all books support their growing understanding (including mathematical understanding) of their world.

Art area

▲ painting and drawing materials
▲ variety of types of paper
▲ dough and clay materials

Art materials as discussed in Chapter 8 allow children to explore a range of mathematical concepts and to begin to represent them symbolically.

Block area

▲ blocks
▲ vehicles, people, animals

Blocks of different weights and sizes give young children an immense range of mathematical experiences. Adding small-world play materials promotes the imaginative play which cements that learning.

TABLE 9.1 *continued*

Arranging and equipping an environment for learning (based on Post and Hohmann 2000)	Supporting mathematical thinking and learning
Home area ▲ dolls and accessories ▲ kitchen furnishings ▲ dishes and utensils (real, not toy) ▲ dress-up clothes and accessories ▲ plants	Exploring texture, size, weight, etc.; making comparisons; increasing physical competence; and developing imagination are all vital elements in becoming a thinker and learner (including a mathematical thinker and learner).
Toy area ▲ things to fit together and take apart ▲ off/on, open/close materials ▲ things for filling and emptying (variety of containers and shells, stones, fabric, chain, etc.) ▲ things for pretend play	The fact that very young children's learning is largely unconscious means that it requires a great deal of repetition (Eliot 1999). However, it also means that once explored and learnt it is very well remembered. Young children love to repeat actions in different contexts, with different materials, to discover why things happen and how things work. To combine all this with the opportunity to play imaginatively is vital to effective learning and thinking.
Outdoors ▲ natural features, e.g. trees, hill ▲ movement materials ▲ things that move in the wind ▲ crawling surfaces ▲ things to climb ▲ things to get inside ▲ swings ▲ sand and water play materials ▲ balls ▲ riding/rocking toys ▲ push and pull toys ▲ loose materials (e.g. paints and paper, chalk, bubble-blowing, beanbags, blankets for tents) ▲ surfaces and boundaries for babies (e.g. blankets, mats, low fences, large bolsters etc.)	All the experiences that children can have indoors should be available outdoors. The contribution to thinking and learning (including mathematical thinking and learning) is equally valid.

mathematical investigations and explorations. Blank board games, dice and spinners (some with numbers and some with dots) were also added.

► Specific and structured maths equipment such as Pattern Blocks for exploring pattern and shape; magnetic numbers, number lines and squares; two- and three-dimensional shapes such as Poleidoblocs for building and tessellating; and calculators.

► Resources for measuring length, weight, capacity and time (such as tape measures, timers, scales, etc.). Resources pertaining to money generally interest young children too – it's something real.

► Some relevant reference books that might include topic-related stories. Lesley Hill, for example (in Marsden and Woodbridge 2005), reports adding *One Snowy Night* (Butterworth 2003) to her maths area along with the penguins, stars and polar bears described above.

► Materials for recording – whiteboards and pens, paper, clipboards, etc.

It is also useful to have some similar maths resources regularly available outdoors. A sectioned box or trolley containing timers and stopwatches; calculators; tape measures and metre sticks; large-scale materials for creating games such as skittles and large dice; and materials for recording, such as clipboards, whiteboards, playground chalk and felt-tip pens.

Additions to general provision, indoors and out

In addition to these specific mathematical resources every area of provision indoors and out should include some resources designed to promote mathematical thinking and learning. Adding resources such as a calendar, a clock, a petty-cash receipt book, and raffle tickets (Worthington and Carruthers 2003) to the writing and drawing area, for example, can enhance children's interest in and enthusiasm for mathematics. Promoting mathematical provision in the role play area might entail adding some materials for a birthday party, or take-away menus and phone books.

Table 9.2 gives some examples of suitable resources to be added to outdoor provision to enhance their mathematical potential.

93

TABLE 9.2 Enhancing outdoor provision to promote mathematical thinking and learning

Importance of outdoor provision	Examples of experiences and activities promoting mathematical understanding and possible additional resources	Aspects of PSRN
Examples of materials or activities that cannot easily be explored indoors	Washing line with lots of pegs and clothes for pegging out (large and small pegs/large and small items of washing)	▲ number ▲ shape, space and measures ▲ pattern ▲ problem-solving ▲ calculation (how many more pegs will we need?)
	Shape, number or pattern walk, using digital cameras to record what has been seen	▲ number, shape or pattern ▲ shape, space and measures
Examples of materials for large-scale activity	Marking out roadways using paint rollers, household brushes and buckets, playground chalk	▲ shape, space and measures ▲ problem-solving
	Parachute games	▲ area, distance, direction, position (opposite, next to, etc.)
Examples of materials for noisy play	Large-scale noisy music and sound-making using dustbin lids, tin mugs, plates, etc. allows children to develop comparative language, explore distances at which sounds can be heard, etc.	▲ shape, space and measures ▲ pattern (large instrument, deep sound)
Taking advantage of natural materials and phenomena	Planting and growing	▲ time ▲ number (how many shall we plant?) ▲ calculation (how many more do you think we need?) ▲ pattern (seasons; planting)
	Weather – exploring puddles and shadows; mark-making in the snow; seeing and feeling the effects of winds of different strengths, outside in the rain with umbrellas and boots; wheeled toy making tracks in puddles; windmills and kites; windchimes	▲ number ▲ shape, space and measures ▲ predicting
	Aspects of the space – slopes, different textured surfaces, paths, hedges, fences	These aspects have much potential for developing mathematical language: ▲ vocabulary ▲ shape, space and measures (including area, perimeter, distance, etc.)
Outdoor role play themes	Builders' merchant; construction site; garage; fire station; train station; ship	The whole maths curriculum – depending on the resources selected

Based on Cartwright et al. 2002; Skinner 2005

Themed provision

Topics or themes that tap into children's individual enthusiasms and interests are an excellent basis for developing mathematical thinking and learning. A focus on pattern, for example, can be highlighted in all areas of provision, enabling children to make connections between different materials and experiences. A child following an interest in rotation might access wheeled vehicles outdoors, in small-world play and in the block area; rotating bases for use in making models; books about vehicles. He or she might also use a plate for drawing and cutting out circles. Outdoors, hoops, tyres and large wooden spools can be rolled. Adult intervention would enable children to talk about the similarities and differences and to develop relevant mathematical vocabulary.

Overall, provision needs to well-organised so that children:

▶ know where to find the materials that will support their mathematical interests;
▶ come across resources that challenge their mathematical assumptions; and
▶ experience a wide range of events and activities that encourage them to approach maths confidently and make connections in their mathematical learning.

Books are an excellent way of drawing experiences together. Providing some books in each area of provision helps to promote the making of connections. As discussed earlier in this chapter, fact and fiction books in the maths corner can encourage children to connect mathematical ideas with other interests. A copy of *Actual Size* (Jenkins 2006) in a science area or the book area will promote a good deal of mathematical discussion and comparison, as well as challenging assumptions. The book has beautiful 'actual size' drawings of the teeth of a great white shark, the foot of an African elephant or the enormous eye of a giant squid. A tiny fish is just 9 millimetres long.

KEY POINTS

Establishing a mathematically rich environment – indoors and out, using imagined and real situations and across all areas of the curriculum and provision – is an essential element of supporting mathematical thinking and learning.

95

Chapter 10

Confident adults supporting confident mathematicians

> To be successful, maths learning needs to involve children in doing, thinking and playing. It should be interactive, ensuring that children are directors of the action as well as enthusiastic participants and that they have time to reflect on what happens.
>
> (Skinner 2005: 7)

In this chapter you will:

▶ explore some strategies for promoting parents' confidence in their mathematical abilities;

▶ consider the importance of confident adults developing mathematical confidence in children;

▶ examine the impact of promoting positive relationships between parents and professionals.

Maths is a subject in which a majority of the population lack confidence. Parents and practitioners often feel that they are not good at maths and therefore may avoid exploring mathematical ideas with children. This chapter makes the case for encouraging staff to feel confident about their own abilities and to help in promoting parents' confidence. In this way, children can be made to feel more confident about themselves as mathematicians.

CONFIDENT PARENTS

There is evidence (see, for example, Young-Loveridge 1989) that families who give mathematics a high profile in their daily lives help children to become what Young-Loveridge terms *young experts*. Gifford (2005, citing Young-Loveridge) draws attention to the similarities seen in such families. *Young expert* mathematicians are likely to come from families where they discuss numbers and time, encourage children to play with coins, calculators, play games involving cards and dice, and where dates of birthdays and other events are noted and anticipated. In addition, these young experts are likely to have some unique interests and abilities too.

> One child collected the money in poker games at family gatherings. Another child was very interested in car speeds, time and distance: his family moved frequently and often discussed car journeys. . . . Seth, whose father kept pigeons . . . (had) conversations about racing, time and distance. . . . A shopkeeper's daughter played at writing long lists of numbers and adding them up. One child with asthma learned to count 30 puffs with her nebulizer. Another knew the weight in kilos of all the members of her family: her mother went to a slimming club and her baby brother was weighed at the clinic. . . .
>
> (Gifford 2005: 33)

The EPPE (Effective Provision of Pre-school Education) project tracked the progress of 3,000 young children through various forms of pre-school provision. As part of that work, researchers sought to identify the effect of the home learning environment on young children's progress (Melhuish *et al.* 2001). They characterise a positive home learning environment as one in which children and parents sing and recite nursery rhymes together, play with numbers, shapes and letters, visit the library, and where there are rich opportunities for painting and drawing. In general, parents in such homes make learning a high profile and enjoyable part of day to day life.

What is especially striking about the EPPE study is that the quality of the home learning environment is highlighted as the variable in the early years that can be seen to have the most lasting effect on children's long-term achievement and progress. In earlier studies, the following have all been regarded as being decisive factors in the learning and progress of young children:

▶ the quality of pre-school education received (see, for example, Sylva *et al.* 1999);
▶ the mother's level of education (see, for example, Tizard and Hughes 1984); or

▶ the socio-economic status of the family (see, for example, Hart and Risley 1995).

Although it is apparent that all of these factors do have an impact on children's subsequent achievement, the EPPE study maintains that the home learning environment has an even greater impact. Desforges (2003) suggests that this is because these parents see themselves as having the ability to help their children. Their confidence, he claims, has a positive effect on the child's own self-image as a learner.

Of course, as we saw in Chapter 1, since most of the population lacks confidence in their mathematical ability, not all parents are able to help their children to be confident mathematicians. Some parents' fear of maths is communicated – often unwittingly – to children. Some parents lack confidence because they think that the way they might go about helping their children to count or calculate will not be seen by professionals as appropriate. Both what counts as mathematics and how it is taught have changed since many parents were at school. What is sad is that many parents who themselves did not succeed at maths when they were at school, all too often expect that their children will (and perhaps should) go through the same experiences that led to their own failure. Some even say that they assume that their children will have the same problems. Others talk of their panic and indicate that they want their children to learn to both enjoy and understand maths (Pound 2006a). What is worrying is that:

▶ children arrive at school with very different levels of mathematical competence;
▶ these differences remain evident throughout primary and secondary school;
▶ the gap between children who achieve well and those who do not is not simply stable but in fact grows larger as children progress through school. Children achieving at lower levels fall further and further behind.

(Bobis *et al.* 2005)

This means that early childhood practitioners have a clear responsibility both:

▶ to help parents understand how they can support their children's mathematical thinking and learning; and
▶ to ensure that they themselves find ways to tackle the inequalities that exist when children arrive in an early years setting.

Helping parents to become more confident about supporting their children's mathematical thinking and learning would appear to be a vital starting point. The Basic Skills Agency report that their family numeracy programmes are effective, both in building parents' confidence and in giving them insight into how their children develop mathematical thinking and learning (Basic Skills Agency 1998).

Parents can be helped to create the positive home learning environment shown by EPPE research to support high levels of achievement on entry to school. The EPPE researchers suggested that parenting groups set up in early years settings were effective in achieving this.

Case Study 2: OCEAN MATHEMATICS FOUNDATION STAGE PILOT PROJECT

The Ocean Mathematics Project is a well-established project in primary and secondary schools in the London Borough of Tower Hamlets, in east London. The project's aims are to enhance parents' and students' confidence and participation in mathematics. In 2005, a pilot project was set up in the foundation stage of a primary school. The aims of the pilot project included:

▶ involving families with helping their youngest children with mathematics by providing resources and inviting parents to workshops;

▶ modelling good practice in early years mathematics;

▶ building on what parents were already doing with their children at home in mathematics;

▶ promoting the enjoyment of mathematics for families and children together.

The workshops were very successful with very high levels of attendance. Each one focused on a different area of mathematics, such as number or time. One session took the shape of a maths walk in the neighbourhood – which was particularly popular with parents. They commented on how pleased they were to have been given so many suggestions for supporting mathematical development while they were undertaking everyday tasks. They were reassured by the fact that so many of these activities took little or no additional time, made interactions with children more enjoyable and helped them to develop mathematical thinking and learning.

Parents took ideas from the workshops for things they could do at home. At each session, maths games were made available for parents and children to use at home. Families were given a book of relevant songs and rhymes. Every child was also equipped with a 'tool kit' which was kept at home. By including scissors, pens and pencils, glue, a clipboard, counting toys, dice, a number line (1–30) and number cards (0–9) in a plastic wallet, the project team ensured that every child or family had the materials that would support mathematical activities.

It is clear from parents' statements that the workshops led them to develop belief in themselves as being able to influence outcomes for their children. The quotes from parents shown below are examples of their determination to try things out at home – thus developing the kind of positive learning environment shown by EPPE research to be so effective in promoting children's motivation to learn:

▶ The best thing is seeing how excited the children are about maths.

▶ The kids have loved the sessions – the way the session is conducted is very exciting.

▶ The workshops are brilliant – it gives them and me confidence to try!

▶ Brilliant! Children learn far more . . . when they enjoy themselves.

▶ I've learnt techniques to help my daughter – I'm already finding new things to do at home.

▶ If there were any more short courses like this then I would love to attend. It helped me and my daughter and gave me an insight of what M does at school.

▶ I'd like more sessions [that] teach parents to teach children.

▶ It has made me more aware of the fact that maths is everywhere.

▶ It has made me think about ways to use maths in everyday situations.

▶ I was able to use the same games with the whole family – boys and girls played together and they don't usually do that.

▶ Before [the workshops] I wasn't really teaching them. The workshops have helped me to see how to help them.

> ▶ I didn't know that maths is everywhere so now I do [I find it in] lots of everyday things.

> ▶ We like the games to take home – the whole family play and she learns such a lot.

> ▶ They really enjoy the nursery rhymes – he heard some of the same ones on television and was so excited.

> (adapted from Pound 2006b)

CONFIDENT PRACTITIONERS

When practitioners lack confidence in their mathematical abilities this has an impact on children and families. It means, for example, that practitioners unsure of their own mathematical ability may:

▶ find it difficult or uncomfortable to answer parents' queries about their children's mathematical development or to explain why maths is approached in particular ways in the setting;

▶ brush off or ignore children's questions about maths in case they come across something they feel unable to answer;

▶ be unwilling to engage with children in the sustained, shared dialogue so vital to the development of mathematical thinking;

▶ avoid in-service training opportunities;

▶ be more likely to fall back on their own (largely unsuccessful) experience of learning mathematics;

▶ be less likely to introduce playful or stimulating experiences, materials or activities for learning and teaching maths;

▶ be more likely to see maths, and therefore present it to children, as facts to be learnt rather than as the enjoyable and lively subject it can (and should) be.

The widening gap in children's mathematical achievement is not, of course, solely the responsibility of parents. There may be very good reasons why parents do not or cannot support their children's learning effectively, but this does not mean that children should suffer. Practitioners, too, must work to ensure that everything possible is done to lay a sound foundation for children's developing mathematical thinking and learning. In a series of studies undertaken in Australia and New Zealand, it was concluded that 'developing confident and capable mathematicians in the early years of schooling' (Bobis *et al.* 2005: 51) requires adults who:

▶ are able to assess children's current mathematical understanding; and
▶ have a clear idea of where they have to get to – their mathematical destination.

Getting to know what children know or have learnt about mathematics at home is vital to making an effective assessment of their understanding. Gifford (2005) reminds us that children's home experiences are very varied and that unless practitioners know something of what children's home experiences are it will be difficult to assess them accurately. Moreover, it will be difficult for children to make connections between what they know at home and what they are being offered in the early years setting.

Gifford (2005: 31) suggests that practitioners 'need to be very knowledgeable about children's home practices, which may be diverse and not very accessible.' She goes on to list some of the experiences that children may have had at home. In addition to what the *young experts* achieved (discussed earlier in this chapter), these experiences may include:

▶ counting on fingers or not counting on fingers. Some children will have been discouraged, whereas others will have been taught some of the many ways of finger counting used in different cultures. Gifford (2005) describes a five-year-old who has been taught to count up to 30 by using a traditional technique counting three to each finger;
▶ informal, playful or everyday activities, such as helping at the supermarket, cooking, etc.;
▶ formal teaching of numbers or even sums;
▶ games such as snakes and ladders;
▶ dot-to-dot books.

Above all, practitioners need to gain sufficient confidence to be able to talk comfortably and knowledgeably to parents about their children's mathematical thinking and learning. Some of that confidence will come from attending in-service training sessions, some from reading books like this! Discussing with colleagues about how they present and answer questions about mathematics (from children and parents) will also support the growth of confidence. But, perhaps more than anything else, working and playing alongside children as they discover maths will help.

PARENTS AND PRACTITIONERS WORKING TOGETHER

Studies of parental involvement in their children's education (see Desforges 2003) stress the fact that children themselves play an active part in making links between home and school or other early years setting. When children are very young this role as mediator can place a great deal of stress on them. Parents and practitioners need to work together to ensure that the burden of trying to make connections between what happens at home and what happens in the early years setting does not fall on children. This means that all the adults involved must find ways to cooperate. This is true of all aspects of children's learning and development – but perhaps the need to work together is particularly important in maths since it is a subject that so many people feel anxious about. Parents and practitioners together can minimise the burden for the child in a number of ways.

The outreach worker on the Ocean Mathematics pilot project commented on the additional stress placed on children when their parents are not familiar with the school system because they have not been educated in this country. She suggested that Ocean Mathematics, by educating parents, was 'lightening the load for the child'. She, as the daughter of an immigrant family herself, empathised with the efforts that these very young children had to make to bridge the gap between home and school. She felt strongly that in familiarising families with the school system, children were being supported.

Not all early years settings face these particular issues and yet many families do not feel comfortable in tackling the mathematics curriculum. Professionals can support children and their families by trying out some of the following strategies:

- ▶ Providing family numeracy sessions or workshops such as those offered by Ocean Mathematics for parents.
- ▶ Lending maths games that families can play together at home.
- ▶ Lending books with a mathematical focus to share at home. BEAM, for example, publish packs of books for young children entitled *Maths Together* (BEAM 1999), which can easily be enjoyed by children and parents together.

► Working with parents to put together some maths sacks – a pack with a book and props to support play and retelling the story. A maths sack to accompany *Kipper's Toybox* (Inkpen 1993) could, for example, include an empty box, six toys and two mice (Featherstone 2005). Many maths sacks are based on number rhymes such as 'Five Currant Buns' and might have a copy of the rhyme, together with some buns (made of baked dough, papier mâché or cloth) and some pennies.

► Curriculum sessions for parents where a member of staff or a visiting expert explains how and why PSRN is approached in the setting. Giving parents the opportunity to ask questions and try out resources such as Beebots or blocks can be very helpful in promoting shared understandings.

► Newsletters, displays or booklets that explain the maths curriculum can also be helpful.

KEY POINTS

Confident practitioners can help to make parents more confident about supporting their own children's mathematical development. Working together, parents and practitioners can lighten the load for children, making for a more secure and consistent mathematical experience.

Conclusion

Throughout this book there have been a number of core themes. Perhaps the most important one is that, in order to be effective, maths learning and teaching must be made more playful. If adults are bored – children will be. If young children's natural love of fun is ignored – they will assume that maths is somehow different and does not fit readily into their view of the world. Having fun is not enough but it is essential. If children learn early to think that maths is dull, it will be difficult to switch them on to it later. Playing comes naturally and it is a vital tool for learning that can be used to enhance the way in which children learn mathematics.

Making it real for children is another theme – real because it connects with their everyday experiences at home, real because it links to their interests, real because it fits with what is known of the way in which children's brains and bodies learn mathematics. What is real for adults, is not always real for children – so adults have to observe, listen and ask questions in order to find out what is real for them. These are their only possible starting points.

Making connections is the way in which humans learn anything and everything and mathematics is no exception. Adults can help children to make connections by ensuring that there are clear links between what happens at home and what is provided in the early years setting. Connections may be made for example between areas of learning and development, perhaps linking:

- ▶ stories and ICT with PSRN;
- ▶ mathematical provision in indoor and outdoor areas;
- ▶ resources and experiences in each area of continuous provision with aspects of PSRN.

Above all, the development of children's mathematical thinking and learning cannot be confined to the maths area or carpet time. It has to underpin all activities and experiences and to be underpinned by confident guessing, self-motivated problem-finding, creative pattern-seeking and abstract thought. Mathematically rich and varied experiences are essential and although maths games, songs and rhymes support the learning they cannot replace real experiences. The time is right to make this area of learning and development, in Steffe's (2004) words, 'the mathematics of children'.

References

Athey, C. (2007) (2nd edn) *Extending Thought in Young Children* London: Paul Chapman.

Basic Skills Agency (1998) *Family Numeracy Adds Up* London: NFER/BSA.

BEAM (1997) *Learning Mathematics in the Nursery: Desirable Approaches* London: BEAM.

BEAM (1999) *Maths Together* London: Walker Books.

BEAM (2003) *Starting Out* London: BEAM.

Bobis, J., Clarke, B., Clarke, D., Thomas, G., Wright, B., Young-Loveridge, J. and Gould, P. (2005) 'Supporting teachers in the development of young children's mathematical thinking: three large scale cases' *Mathematics Education Research Journal* 16 (3): 27–57.

Bresler, L. (2004) *Knowing bodies, moving minds* Dordrecht: Kluwer Academic Publishers.

Bromley, H. (2005) *50 Exciting Ideas for Developing Maths through Stories* Birmingham: Lawrence Educational Publications.

Bruner, J. (1986) *Actual Minds: Possible Worlds* London: Harvard University Press.

Butterworth, B. (2005) 'The development of arithmetical abilities' *Journal of Child Psychology and Psychiatry* 46: 1003–18.

Cartwright, P., Scott, K. and Stevens, J. (2002) *A Place to Learn* London: LEARN (Lewisham Early Years Advice and Resource Network).

Claxton, G. (1997) *Hare Brain, Tortoise Mind* London: Fourth Estate.

Clements, D. H. (1998) *Geometric and Spatial Thinking in Young Children* http://eric.ed.gov/ERICDocs/data/ericdocs259/content_storage_01/0000019b/80/15/f7/3c.pdf (ED436232) (accessed 10 September 2007).

Desforges, C. (2003) *The Impact of Parental Involvement, Parental Support and Family Education on Pupil Achievement and Adjustment* London: DfES Research Report No. 433.

Devi, S. (1990) *Figuring* London: Penguin.

Devlin, K. (2000) *The Maths Gene* London: Weidenfeld & Nicolson.

DfES (2007) *Practice Guidance for the Early Years Foundation Stage non-statutory guidance* Nottingham: DfES Publications.

Doman, G. and Doman, J. (1994) *How to Teach Your Baby Math* New York: Avery Publishing Group.

Donaldson, M. (1986) *Children's Minds* London: HarperCollins.

Durkin, D. (2001) *Thinking Together: Quality Adult Children Interactions* Wellington, NZ: NZCER.

Early Childhood Mathematics Group (1997) *Learning Mathematics in the Nursery* London: BEAM.

Egan, K. (1988) *Teaching as Storytelling* London: Routledge.

Egan, K. (1989) *Primary Understanding* London: Routledge.

Eliot, L. (1999) *Early Intelligence* London: Penguin Books.

Featherstone, S. (2005) *The Little Book of Maths from Stories* Lutterworth: Featherstone Education.

Fisher, R. (1995) *Teaching Children to Think* Cheltenham: Stanley Thornes.

Gardner, H. (1983) *Frames of Mind: the Theory of Multiple Intelligences* New York: Basic Books.

Gardner, H. (1993) *The Unschooled Mind* London: Fontana.

Gardner, H. (1999) *Intelligence Reframed* London: Basic Books.

Gardner, H. (2006) *Five Minds for the Future* Boston, MA: Harvard Business School Press.

Gerhardt, S. (2004) *Why Love Matters* London: Brunner-Routledge.

Gifford, S. (2005) *Teaching Mathematics 3–5* Maidenhead: Open University Press.

Goldschmied, E. and Selleck, D. (1996) *Communication between Babies in their First Year* London: National Children's Bureau.

Goleman, D. (1996) *Emotional Intelligence* London: Fontana.

Gopnik, A., Meltzoff, A. and Kuhl, P. (1999) *How Babies Think* London: Weidenfeld & Nicolson.

Gura, P. (1992) *Exploring Learning: Young Children and Block Play* London: Paul Chapman.

Hall, N. and Martello, J. (1996) (eds) *Listening to Children Think* London: Hodder & Stoughton.

Hart, B. and Risley, T. (1995) *Meaningful Differences* Baltimore, MA: Paul Brookes Publishing.

Healy, J. (1999) *Failure to Connect* New York: Touchstone.

Hobson, P. (2002) *The Cradle of Thought* London: Macmillan.

Inhelder, B. and Piaget, J. (1958) *The Growth of Logical Thinking* London: Routledge & Kegan Paul.

Jenkinson, S. (2001) *The Genius of Play* Stroud, Glos.: Hawthorn Press.

Lee, T. and Tompsett, I. (2004) *Dramatic Mathematics: Teachers Resource Pack* London: MakeBelieve Arts/Creating Success EiC Action Zone LB of Lewisham.

Lee, T. and Pound, L. (2005) *Creative Approaches to Mathematics* London: Make Believe Arts.

Livingstone, T. (2005) *Child of Our Time* London: Bantam Press.

Lucas, B. (2001) *Power up Your Mind* London: Nicholas Brealey Publishing.

MacGregor, H. (1998) *Tom Thumb's Musical Maths* London: A&C Black.

MacGregor, H. and Gargrave, B. (2001) *Let's go, Zudie-o* London: A&C Black.

MacGregor, H. and Gargrave, B. (2004) *Let's go Shoolie-shoo* London: A&C Black.

Macnamara, A. (1996) 'From Home to School – do Children Preserve their Counting skills' in Broadhead, P. (ed.) *Researching the Early Years Continuum* Clevedon: Multilingual Matters.

MakeBelieve Arts (2007) *The Woman who Cooked Everything* London: MakeBelieve Arts.

Malaguzzi, L. (1995) 'History, Ideas and Basic Philosophy' in Edwards, C., Gandini, L. and Forman, G. (eds) *The Hundred Languages of Children* Norwood, NJ: Ablex Publishing Corporation.

Marsden, L. and Woodbridge, J. (2005) *Looking closely at learning and teaching: a journey of development* Huddersfield: Early Excellence.

Matthews, J. (2003) (2nd edn) *Drawing and Painting: Children and Visual Representation* London: Paul Chapman Publishing.

Mazur, B. (2003) *Imagining numbers* London: Penguin Books.

Meek, M. (1985) 'Play and Paradoxes; Some Considerations of Imagination and Language' in Wells, G. and Nicholls, J. (eds) *Language and Learning: an Interactional Perspective* Lewes, East Sussex: Falmer Press.

Melhuish, E., Sylva, K., Siraj-Blatchford, I. and Taggart, B. (2001) *Technical paper 7: Social, behavioural and cognitive development at 3–4 years relative to family background. Report from the Effective Provision of Pre-school education research* London: Institute of Education, University of London.

Miles, R. (1994) *The Children we Deserve* London: HarperCollins.

Montague-Smith, A. (2002) (2nd edn) *Mathematics in Nursery Education* London: David Fulton.

Moyles, J. (1989) *Just Playing?* Milton Keynes: Open University Press.

Moyles, J. and Adams, S. (2001) *StEPS: Statements of Entitlement to Play: A Framework for Playful Teaching 3–7 Year Olds* Buckingham, Open University Press.

Nadel, J. and Butterworth, G. (1999) *Imitation in Infancy* Cambridge: Cambridge University Press.

Paley, V. G. (1981) *Wally's Stories* Cambridge, MA: Harvard University Press.

Paley, V. G. (1990) *The Boy Who Would be a Helicopter* London: Harvard University Press.

Piaget, J. (1952) *The Origin of Intelligence in the Child* London: Routledge & Kegan Paul.

Post, J. and Hohmann, M. (2000) *Tender Care and Early Learning* Ypsilanti, MI: High/Scope Press.

Pound, L. (2006a) *Supporting Mathematical Development in the Early Years* Maidenhead: Open University Press.

Pound, L. (2006b) *Ocean Mathematics Project: Evaluation of Foundation Stage Pilot Project 2005–6* Unpublished paper.

Pound, L. and Harrison, C. (2003) *Supporting Musical Development in the Early Years* Buckingham: Open University Press.

QCA (Qualification and Curriculum Authority) (2000) *Curriculum Guidance for the Foundation Stage* London: DfEE/QCA.

Ramachandran, V. S. (2003) *A Brief Tour of Human Consciousness* New York: PI Press.

Ramachandran, V. S. and Blakeslee, S. (1999) *Phantoms in the Brain* London: Fourth Estate.

Rogoff, B. (2003) *The Cultural Nature of Human Development* Oxford: Oxford University Press.

Sammons, P., Sylva, K., Melhuish, E., Siraj-Blatchford, I., Taggart, B. and Elliot, K. (2002) *Measuring the Impact of Pre-school on Children's Cognitive Progress over the Pre-school Period* London: The Institute of Education University of London.

Schiro, M. S. (2004) *Oral Storytelling and Teaching Mathematics* London: Sage.

Siegel, D. (1999) *The Developing Mind* New York: Guilford Press.

Skinner, C. (2005) *Maths Outdoors* London: BEAM.

Steffe, L. (2004) 'PSSM (Principles and Standards for School Mathematics) From a Constructivist Perspective' in Clements, D. H. and Sarama, J. (eds) *Engaging Young Children in Mathematics* London: Lawrence Erlbaum Associates.

Sure Start Unit (2002) *Birth to Three Matters* London: DfES.

Sylva, K., Siraj-Blatchford, I., Melhuish, E., Sammons, P., Taggart, B., *et al.* (1999) *Characteristics of Pre-school Environments* (EPPE Project) London: Institute of Education.

Tizard, B. and Hughes, M. (1984) *Young Children Learning* London: Fontana.

Walsh, D. J. (2004) 'Frog Boy and the American Monkey: the Body in Japanese Schooling' in Bresler, L. (ed.) *Knowing Bodies, Moving Minds* Dordrecht: Kluwer Academic Press.

Whitin, D. and Wilde, S. (1995) *It's the Story that Counts – More Children's Books for Mathematical Learning, K-6* London: Heinemann.

Worthington, M. and Carruthers, E. (2003) *Children's Mathematics: Making Marks, Making Meaning* London: Paul Chapman Publishing.

Young-Loveridge, J. (1989) 'The relationship between children's home experiences and the mathematical skills on entry to school' *Early Child Development and Care* 43: 43–59.

Children's books

Alborough, J. (2004) *Where's my Teddy?* London: Walker Books.

Allen, P. (1988) *Who Sank the Boat?* London: Puffin Books.

Andreae, G. and Sharratt, N. (2007) *Pants* London: Picture Corgi Books.

Bartram, S. (2002) *Man on the Moon* London: Templar Publishing.

Boynton, S. (2000) *Hippos go Berserk* London: Simon & Schuster.

Brown, R. (2000) *Snail Trail* London: Andersen Press.

Browne, E. (1995) *Handa's Surprise* London: Walker Books.

Burningham, J. (1992) *Come Away from the Water Shirley* London: Red Fox.

Butterworth, N. (2003) *The Secret Path* London: Picture Lions.

Butterworth, N. (2003) *The Treasure Hunt* London: Picture Lions.

Butterworth, N. (2003) *One Snowy Night* London: Picture Lions.

Campbell, R. (1985) *Dear Zoo* London: Picture Puffin.

Clement, R. (1995) *Counting on Frank* Boston, MA: Houghton Mifflin.

Cowell, C. and Ellis, A. (2001) *One Too Many Tigers* London: Hodder Children's Books.

Dunbar, J. and Dunbar, P. (2005) *Shoe Baby* London: Walker Books.

Freedman, C. and Cort, B. (2007) *Aliens Love Underpants* London: Simon and Schuster.

Inkpen, M. (1993) *Kipper's Toybox* London: Hodder Children's Books.

Inkpen, M. (2006) *The Blue Balloon* London: Hodder Children's Books.

Inkpen, M. (2006) *The Great Pet Sale* London: Hodder Children's Books.

Jenkins, S. (2006) *Actual Size* London: Frances Lincoln Children's Books.

Kerr, J. (2006) *The Tiger Who Came to Tea* London: HarperCollins Children's Books.

Latimer, M. (2007) *Shrinking Sam* Cambridge, MA: Barefoot Books.

Luciani, B. and Tharlet, E. (2003) *How Will we Get to the Beach?* London: Michael Neugebauer Books.

Rosen, M. and Oxenbury, H. (1993) *We're Going on a Bear Hunt* London: Walker Books.

Sayre, A. and Sayre, J. (2004) *One is a Snail and Ten is a Crab* London: Walker Books.

Stickland, P. (1997) *Ten Terrible Dinosaurs* Andover: Ragged Bears Publishing.

Whybrow, I. and Reynolds, A. (2003) *Harry and the Robots* London: Puffin Books.

Wilson, A. and Bartlett, A. (2002) *Over in the Grasslands* London: Macmillan Children's Books.

Index